THE
LARK RISE
RECIPE
BOOK

MARY NORWAK

SELECT
EDITIONS

ACKNOWLEDGEMENTS

Colour paintings

FRONTISPIECE: *The Harvesters* by George Vicat Cole – Wolverhampton Art Gallery/Bridgeman Art Library; p.6 *Market Day* by H. C. Bryant – Fine Art Photographic Library; p.8 *The New Brood* by Alfred Provis – Fine Art Photographic Library; p.14 *Picking Turnips* by Robert Cree Crawford – Fine Art Photographic Library; p.26 *The Intruder* by William Weekes – Fine Art Photographic Library; p.40 *Helping to Make Blackberry Pie* by Edith Hayllar Phillips/Bridgeman Art Library; p.60 *Fresh from the Orchard* by Frederick Daniel Hardy – Fine Art Photographic Library; p.82 *Picking Blackberries* by Myles Birket Foster – Fine Art Photographic Library; p.93 *The Christmas Visitors* by Frederick Daniel Hardy – Wolverhampton Art Gallery/Bridgeman Art Library; p.108 *Domestic Lesson* by Arthur Claude Cooke – Gavin Graham Gallery/Bridgeman Art Library; p.116 *Sickness of Health* by William Hemsley – Fine Art Photographic Library; p.120 *Baby's Birthday* by Frederick Daniel Hardy – Wolverhampton Art Gallery/Bridgeman Art Library.

The woodcut engravings are by Thomas Bewick.

This edition published 1992
by the Promotional Reprint Company Limited,
for Selecta Book Limited,
Devizes, UK.
and exclusively for
Angus & Robertson Bookshops in Australia

ISBN 1 85648 084 4

Printed in Hong Kong

THE
LARK RISE
RECIPE
BOOK

Contents

Introduction

Flora Thompson was born in a cottage in a tiny hamlet in north Oxfordshire in 1877. She was brought up in poverty, but she was a natural reporter, and her skill in recording country life a hundred years ago has ensured her fame. Her best known work is the trilogy *Lark Rise to Candleford* which describes life during the last twenty years of the nineteenth century, but she also wrote a fictional account of the same period under the title *Still Glides the Stream*. She later lived in southern England and finally in Devonshire, and continued writing essays and poetry, and made a series of contributions to a small magazine, *The Catholic Fireside*, many of which have been collected under the title *A Country Calendar*.

From these five books, I have drawn together her vivid descriptions of the domestic life of country people in the time of our grandparents and great-grandparents, mostly seen through the eyes of the fictional small girl Laura, who was in many respects a portrait of Flora Thompson herself. All her impressions were collected by the time she was fourteen, and her descriptions enable us to know what the sight, sound and smell of country life was like at the end of the nineteenth century. From Flora Thompson we know exactly how country women managed their impoverished households, what their husbands grew in the gardens, how they prepared their food and homely remedies and how they passed their meagre leisure time. We can share with her the joys of mushrooming and blackberrying, the preparation of the family pig, the gleaning of surplus wheat at harvest time, and the simple joy of a Christmas so different from the modern over-blown festival.

Because her reporting is so vivid, it has been possible to collect together contemporary recipes from manuscripts of the period and to know exactly how the meals of the period were created and how they tasted. Most of the dishes are very simple and very good, cheap to prepare and delicious to eat, and this is the real food which our ancestors enjoyed and which today's cooks are beginning to seek again. All the recipes for main course dishes and puddings will serve 4-6 people, depending on their appetites.

The Lark Rise Kitchen

"On the morning of the harvest home dinner everybody prepared themselves for a tremendous feast, some to the extent of going without breakfast, that the appetite might not be impaired. And what a feast it was! Such a bustling in the farmhouse kitchen for days beforehand; such boiling of hams and roasting of sirloins; such a stacking of plum puddings, made by the Christmas recipe; such a tapping of eighteen-gallon casks and baking of plum loaves would astonish those accustomed to the appetites of today. By noon the whole parish had assembled, the workers and their wives and children to feast and the sprinkling of the better-to-do to help with the serving. The only ones absent were the aged bedridden and their attendants, and to them, the next day, portions, carefully graded in daintiness according to their social standing, were carried by the children from the remnants of the feast. A plum pudding was considered a delicate compliment to an equal of the farmer; slices of beef or ham went to the 'bettermost poor' [those who worked but still failed to make a proper living]; and a hambone with plenty of meat left upon it or part of a pudding or a can of soup to the commonalty.

Long tables were laid out of doors in the shade of a barn, and soon after twelve o'clock the cottagers sat down to the good cheer, with the farmer carving at the principal table, his wife with her tea urn at another, the daughters of the house and their friends circling the tables with vegetable dishes and beer jugs, and the grandchildren, in their stiff, white, embroidered frocks, dashing hither and thither to see that everybody had what they required. As a background there was the rick-yard with its new yellow stacks and, over all, the mellow sunshine of late summer."

——— *Lark Rise*, Chapter 15

This is the perfect picture of life in the English countryside one hundred years ago, but Laura's father, who was a "tradesman" and did not have a share of the harvest feast, saw that such a sunlit celebration masked great poverty. He used to say that "the farmer paid his men starvation wages all the year and thought he made it up to them by giving that one good meal".

Most of the village families had just ten shillings (50p) – which would have been about a quarter of their income – for their food each week, and there was a local saying that "poverty's no disgrace, but 'tis a great inconvenience". The older people often had good pieces of furniture, china and silver, left from the days when the countryside was prosperous, but in the 1880s farming was in decline, and the rural population was very poor, though all too rich in children.

"In their houses the good, solid, hand-made furniture of their forefathers had given place to the cheap and ugly products of the early machine age. A deal table, the top ribbed and softened by much scrubbing; four or five windsor chairs with the varnish blistered and flaking; a side table for the family photographs and ornaments, and a few stools for fireside seats, together with the beds upstairs, made up the collection spoken of by its owners as 'our few sticks of furniture'."

——— *Lark Rise*, Chapter 6

The kitchen of such houses was often the only living-room, and sometimes it had to serve as a bedroom as well. The walls were whitewashed, or covered with brightly coloured flowered wallpaper or pasted-up newspapers. Grocers' calendars were framed to serve as pictures.

"Yet, even out of these unpromising materials, in a room which was kitchen, living-room, nursery, and wash-house combined, some women would contrive to make a pleasant, attractive-looking home. A well-whitened hearth, a home-made rag rug in bright colours, and a few geraniums on the window-sill would cost nothing, but make a great difference to the general effect. Others despised these finishing touches. What was the good of breaking your back pegging rugs for the children to mess up when an old sack thrown down would serve the same purpose, they said. As to flowers in pots, they didn't hold with the nasty, messy things. But they did, at least, believe in cleaning up their houses once a day, for public opinion demanded that of them. There were plenty of bare, comfortless homes in the hamlet, but there was not one really dirty one."

——— *Lark Rise*, Chapter 6

While the women always did all their own housework and cooked family meals, many of them were desperate to earn a little extra money. In earlier times, tough "field women" had formed gangs to work on the land, picking up stones, topping turnips, hoeing and mending sacks, but they were lawless, wild creatures, notorious for being slatternly and having large families of illegitimate children. These women had such a bad reputation that few countrywomen wanted to do field work, but some of the respectable older women with grown-up families worked in the fields from ten to four, with an hour off for a meal. They worked in "sunbonnets, hobnailed boots and men's coats, with coarse aprons of sacking enveloping the lower part of their bodies". One wore a pair of her husband's corduroy trousers, and others used old trouser legs as gaiters. For heavy farm work in all but the very worst weather, they earned four shillings (20p) each week.

Self-sufficiency was the watchword and everybody who could kept a pig and a large vegetable garden, and sometimes a row of beehives. One of the more comfortable houses belonged to Old Sally and her husband Dick.

"Excepting the inn, it was the largest house in the hamlet, and of the two downstairs rooms one was used as a kind of kitchen-storeroom, with pots and pans and a big red crockery water vessel at one end, and potatoes in sacks and peas and beans spread out to dry at the other. The apple crop was stored on racks suspended beneath the ceiling and bunches of herbs dangled below. In one corner stood the big brewing copper in which Sally still brewed with good malt and hops once a quarter. The scent of the last brewing hung over the place till the next and mingled with apple and onion and dried thyme and

sage smells, with a dash of soap-suds thrown in, to compound the aroma which remained in the children's memories for life . . . "
— *Lark Rise*, Chapter 5

Like all the men of the village, Dick worked hard in his garden. The men were helped by good soil and plenty of manure from their pigsties, but they constantly kept the soil on the move with the hoe, or "tickled" it to make the crops grow. Water for the gardens had to be fetched from the brook a quarter of a mile away. The allotments were divided into two parts, one half for potatoes and the other half for wheat or barley.

"The garden was reserved for green vegetables, currant and gooseberry bushes, and a few old-fashioned flowers. Proud as they were of their celery, peas and beans, cauliflowers and marrows, and fine as were the specimens they could show of these, their potatoes were their special care, for they had to grow enough to last the year round. They grew all the old-fashioned varieties – ashleaf kidney, early rose, American rose, magnum bonum, and the huge misshapen white elephant. Everybody knew the elephant was an unsatisfactory potato, that it was awkward to handle when paring and that it boiled down to a white pulp in cooking; but it produced tubers of such astonishing size that none of the men could resist the temptation to plant it. Every year specimens were taken to the inn to be weighed on the only pair of scales in the hamlet, then handed round for guesses to be made of the weight. As the men said, when a patch of elephants was dug up and spread out, 'You'd got summat to put in your eye and look at.'"
— *Lark Rise*, Chapter 3

This simple garden produce was the basis of all meals, for very little food was actually bought. The family pig provided fresh meat once a year, and bacon and hams for the rest of the time, but "butcher's meat" was virtually unknown except for a joint of beef at Christmas or wedding celebrations. A few chickens were usually kept for eggs and when they had grown old, the birds were boiled or made into puddings; only the better-off had young roasting chickens. There might be rabbits or poached game, and there were also mushrooms and berries picked from the wild. Gooseberries, currants, rhubarb, apples and different types of plums provided sweeter food.

The women gleaned enough corn at harvest to be made into flour which was used for the endless suet puddings which supplemented their diet, and for a few very simple cakes and biscuits. Bread was bought three times a week from the travelling baker, but pies were almost unknown because few cottages had ovens, and most pies had to be taken to the village bakehouse for finishing.

Honey was used instead of sugar, and butter and milk were considered much too expensive for everyday use. Home-made lard was spread on bread and used for cooking, or there might be dripping from the occasional roast pork. Tea cost five shillings (25p) a lb, about half the weekly food allowance, while coffee and chocolate were unknown to the village folk. Their main purchases were small quantities of dried fruit, lumps of sugar which had to be broken small, black treacle, vinegar and salt. Eggs were highly seasonal and could cost as much as twenty old pence (8p) a dozen, while most people could rarely afford fish except for the occasional herring or bloater.

When Laura went to her first job in 1899, the South African war was in progress and would shortly send prices up to a level from which they would never decline. She earned £1 a week, but the price of food had risen greatly since her childhood, and fresh farm butter cost one shilling (5p) a lb, and best bacon rashers eightpence (3p) a lb. She was able to take advantage of a ninepenny (4p) dinner from the local inn which consisted of a thick cut off the joint, two or more vegetables, and a wedge of fruit tart or a round of roly-poly, and this must have seemed luxury after the meals of her childhood.

In her new home at the Candleford Post Office, she was able to enjoy a rather grander kitchen with its big fire and cauldron for boiling the meat, vegetables and puddings than the one in which she had grown up.

"The kitchen was a large room with a flagstone floor and two windows beneath which stood a long, solid-looking table large enough to accommodate the whole household at mealtimes. The foreman and three young unmarried smiths lived in the house, and each of these had his own place at table. Miss Lane, in a higher chair than the others, known as a carving-chair, sat enthroned at the head of the table, then, on the side facing the windows, came Laura and Matthew, the foreman, with a long space of tablecloth between them supposed to be reserved for visitors. Laura's seeming place of honour had, no doubt, been allotted to her for handiness in passing cups and plates. The young smiths sat three abreast at the bottom end of the table and Zillah, the maid, had a small side-table of her own. All meals excepting tea were taken in this order.

Cooking and washing-up were done in the back kitchen; the front kitchen was the family living- and dining-room. In the fireplace a small sitting-room grate with hobs had replaced the fire on the hearth of a few years before; but the open chimney and chimney-corners had been left, and from one of these a long, high-backed settle ran out into the room. In the space thus enclosed a red-and-black carpet had been laid to accommodate Miss Lane's chair at the head of the table and a few fireside chairs. This little room within a room was known as the hearthplace. Beyond it the stone floor was bare but for a few mats.

Brass candlesticks and a brass pestle and mortar ornamented the high mantelshelf, and there were brass warming-pans on the walls, together with a few coloured prints."

—— *Candleford Green*, Chapter 1

The village of Candleford was large enough to support a number of tradesmen, including a draper and grocer. It was a matter of principle among the middle classes to support these shops and they did not dream of shopping further afield to save a few shillings. Where there were more than two shops of a kind in the village, it was the custom to patronise them alternately. All the tradesmen expected to deliver their wares.

The baker, the butcher and the grocer were the main providers. The butcher bought his animals at the local market, hung the meat himself and butchered the carcasses, keeping the scrag ends and scraps for his poorer customers. The grocer had to weigh out all his goods, blend them and pack each individual item, and he was directly responsible for quality to his customers. The grocer and his wife lived in comfort above their mahogany-countered shop, but they were generous and allowed unlimited credit to poor families, as well as slipping tasty oddments into their baskets. As well as the more prosperous shops, there were cottages with little front rooms occupied by old ladies who sold gingerbread and boiled sweets, or even penny platefuls of cooked prunes and rice. Another individual trader was the muffin man:

> "Polly was toasting muffins before a huge fire. She had been on her favourite Saturday-afternoon errand to waylay the muffin man, who once a week on that day at that season came through the village with his wares in a flat oil-cloth-covered tray on his head, ringing his bell and calling, 'Muffins and crumpets! Who'll buy! Who'll buy! Muffins and crumpets and S-a-a-l-l-y L-u-n-n-s!' A covered soup-plate containing those she had toasted stood to keep hot on the high steel fender. Firelight gleamed on the walls and ceiling and picked out with its flickering light the brass candlesticks and the crockery on the dresser."
>
> —— *Still Glides the Stream*, Chapter 10

Here was the full range of the poor and middling folk in the deep countryside at the end of the nineteenth century, self-sufficient and struggling to manage without ovens, gas or electricity, running water or cleaning equipment, yet appreciating the good and simple things of life.

> "But, in spite of their poverty and the worry and anxiety attending it, they were not unhappy, and, though poor, there was nothing sordid about their lives. 'The nearer the bone the sweeter the meat,' they used to say, and they were getting very near the bone from which their country ancestors had fed. Their children and children's children would have to depend wholly upon whatever was carved for them from the communal joint, and for their pleasure upon the mass enjoyments of a new era. But for that generation there was still a small picking left to supplement the weekly wage. They had their home-cured bacon, their 'bit o' leazings' [gleanings of corn gathered after the harvest], their small wheat or barley patch on the allotment; their knowledge of herbs for their homely simples, and the wild fruits and berries of the countryside for jam, jellies, and wine, and round about them as part of their lives were the last relics of country customs and the last echoes of country songs, ballads, and game rhymes. This last picking, though meagre, was sweet."
>
> —— *Lark Rise*, Chapter 1

Main Meals

"How was it done on ten shillings a week? Well, for one thing, food was much cheaper than it is today. Then, in addition to the bacon, all vegetables, including potatoes, were home-grown and grown in abundance. The men took great pride in their gardens and allotments and there was always competition amongst them as to who should have the earliest and choicest of each kind. Fat green peas, broad beans as big as a halfpenny, cauliflowers a child could make an armchair of, runner beans and cabbage and kale, all in their seasons went into the pot with the roly-poly and slip of bacon.

Then they ate plenty of green food, all home-grown and freshly pulled; lettuce and radishes and young onions with pearly heads and leaves like fine grass. A few slices of bread and home-made lard, flavoured with rosemary, and plenty of green food 'went down good' as they used to say."

—— Lark Rise, Chapter 1

Meals had to be very simple in the country a hundred years ago for wages were low and families were large. Butcher's meat (as it is still called in the country to this day) was rarely seen, and a joint of beef only appeared as a gift from a farmer at Christmas or wedding feasts. The main meat supply was the family pig, shared with neighbours each year, who would in their turn share their own pig. Home-cured bacon was eaten almost daily, supplemented by the occasional chicken or rabbit. Large quantities of vegetables were eaten, and the meal was completed by a filling suet pudding.

"Here, then, were the three chief ingredients of the one hot meal a day, bacon from the flitch, vegetables from the garden, and flour for the roly-poly. This meal, called 'tea', was taken in the evening, when the men were home from the fields and the children from school, for neither could get home at midday.

About four o'clock, smoke would go up from the chimneys, as the fire was made up and the big iron boiler, or the three-legged pot, was slung on the hook of the chimney-chain. Everything was cooked in the one utensil; the square of bacon, amounting to little more than a taste each; cabbage, or other green vegetables, in one net, potatoes in another, and the roly-poly swathed in a cloth. It sounds a haphazard method in these days of gas and electric cookers; but it answered its purpose, for, by carefully timing the putting in of each item and keeping the simmering of the pot well regulated, each item was kept intact and an appetising meal was produced. The water in which the food had been cooked, the potato parings, and other vegetable trimmings were the pig's share."

—— Lark Rise, Chapter 1

This method of cooking meant that most meat was boiled, and a simple dish like boiled chicken and boiled pork or ham was considered a great delicacy with all the accompanying vegetables.

Chicken in the Pot

3½-4 lb CHICKEN
WATER OR STOCK
1 BAY LEAF
2 lb CARROTS
2 lb TURNIPS
2 lb POTATOES
1 CABBAGE
1 oz BUTTER
1 oz PLAIN FLOUR
SALT AND PEPPER

1 · Put the chicken into a thick, heavy pan and cover with water or stock. Add the bay leaf. Bring to the boil, cover and simmer for 1 hour.

2 · Peel the carrots, turnips and potatoes. Leave them whole if they are small, but otherwise cut in quarters. Add to the chicken and continue cooking for 20 minutes, or until the vegetables are tender.

3 · Cut the cabbage into 8 sections and add to the chicken. Continue cooking for 15 minutes.

4 · Lift the chicken on to a dish and surround with the vegetables.

5 · Melt the butter, stir in the flour and cook gently for 1 minute. Stir in 1 pint chicken cooking liquid, and stir over low heat until creamy.

6 · Season well and pour a little of the sauce over the chicken, serving the rest separately.

Roast chicken was reserved for special days like the Whit Monday Embley Feast described in *Still Glides the Stream* when Charity visited the prosperous blacksmith's house:

> "Then huge dishes of roast fowls and ham and vegetables were brought in and they all sat down to a substantial meal, talking and laughing happily . . .
>
> 'Just another teeny-weeny shaving of ham, Mr. Milton? As I always say, a fowl's not worth eating without it; and, Bess, my dear, you're not getting on at all well. Let me give you another slice off the breast and a spoonful of stuffing?'"

—— *Still Glides the Stream*, Chapter 9

Country Herbed Chicken

3½-4 lb CHICKEN
4 oz BUTTER
1 TABLESPOON CHOPPED FRESH PARSLEY
2 TEASPOONS CHOPPED FRESH THYME
2 TEASPOONS CHOPPED FRESH ROSEMARY
2 TEASPOONS CHOPPED FRESH MARJORAM
GRATED RIND OF 1 LEMON
SALT AND PEPPER

1 · Cream the butter and mix with the herbs, lemon rind, salt and pepper. Spread the mixture over the chicken and put any surplus inside the bird.

2 · Roast in a moderate oven (350°F/180°C/Gas Mark 4) for 1½ hours.
3 · Serve with vegetables and, if liked, with slices of freshly boiled bacon.

For a more filling dish, a herb stuffing may be used:
1 · Melt 1 oz butter and cook 1 small finely chopped onion until soft and golden.
2 · Add to 3 oz breadcrumbs, the grated rind and juice of 1 lemon, salt, pepper, 1 tablespoon each of chopped fresh thyme and marjoram, 2 teaspoons chopped fresh parsley and 1 egg.
3 · Stuff the bird and allow 10 minutes extra cooking time.

"Fresh meat was a luxury only seen in a few of the cottages on Sunday, when sixpenny-worth of pieces would be bought to make a meat pudding. If a small joint came their way as a Saturday night bargain, those without oven grates would roast it by suspending it on a string before the fire, with one of the children in attendance as turnspit. Or a 'pot-roast' would be made by placing the meat with a little lard or other fat in an iron saucepan and keeping it well shaken over the fire. But, after all, as they said, there was nothing to beat a 'toad'. For this the meat was enclosed whole in a suet crust and well boiled, a method which preserved all the delicious juices of the meat and provided a good pudding into the bargain."

—— *Lark Rise*, Chapter 1

Pot Roast Lamb Shoulder

1 BONED AND ROLLED LAMB SHOULDER
2 CELERY STICKS
1 LARGE ONION
2 MEDIUM CARROTS
SALT AND PEPPER
1 oz LARD OR DRIPPING
¼ PINT WATER OR STOCK

1 · Tie the lamb into a neat shape.

2 · Chop the celery into 1 in. pieces. Cut the onion into quarters and then cut across each piece to make 8 chunky pieces. Slice the carrots.

3 · Season the surface of the lamb with salt and pepper.

4 · Melt the fat and brown the meat on all sides in a heavy pan. Lift out of the pan and keep on one side.

5 · Brown the vegetables lightly in the fat. Put the meat on top and add the water or stock. Cover tightly and cook over very low heat for 2½ hours.

6 · Slice the lamb and arrange on a warm serving dish. Surround with vegetables and pour over the juices from the pan.

At the vicarage, meat was more plentiful, and it was traditional to roast a large joint on Saturday or Sunday which was then eaten for each meal of the week until the next weekend came round. Beef was particularly popular, closely followed by leg of mutton. The vicar's old servant in *Still Glides the Stream* laments the ways of the new housekeeper:

> "'That 'ooman's fair starvin' the master,' he told people. 'In my time we got a good leg o' mutton or a round o' beef and I roast 'en on Saturday to last th' week, cut an' come again, and there wer' allus a bit o' good wholesome victuals in the place, and ready whenever he might fancy a cut.'"
>
> —— *Still Glides the Stream*, Chapter 8

The Victorian way of cooking beef was to cook it on a spit or hook in front of a good fire, with the meat hanging about 18 inches from the heat. A dripping pan was placed underneath and the meat was basted every twenty minutes until done. The joint was cooked for 15 minutes per lb, and about 20 minutes before it was done, the meat was sprinkled with salt and flour, the fire was roared up, and the meat was turned until brown and crisp on the outside. Gravy was made from the juices in the dripping pan, in which the Yorkshire Pudding was traditionally made.

This kind of joint was always used for the main Christmas meal, and if possible it was served for weddings, followed by plum pudding. Sometimes salt beef was available, and this was popular because it could be cooked with plenty of vegetables and dumplings.

Boiled Beef and Carrots

3 lb SALT BEEF BRISKET
8 oz ONIONS
8 oz CARROTS
6 PEPPERCORNS
SPRIG OF PARSLEY
SPRIG OF THYME
1 BAY LEAF
Dumplings
6 oz PLAIN FLOUR
3 oz SHREDDED SUET
1½ TEASPOONS BAKING POWDER
1 TEASPOON SALT
1 TEASPOON CHOPPED FRESH MIXED HERBS

1 · Soak the meat overnight in cold water.

2 · Drain well and put into a large heavy saucepan. Cover with cold water, bring to the boil and skim well.

3 · Cut the onions and carrots in quarters and put them into the pan with the peppercorns and herbs. Cover the pan and simmer for 2½ hours.

4 · Make the dumplings by mixing together all the ingredients and adding enough cold water to make a stiff dough. Divide the dough into 8 pieces and form each one into a ball.

5 · Add the dumplings to the pan, cover and simmer for 20 minutes.

6 · Serve the beef sliced, with the vegetables and dumplings, and some of the cooking liquid.

"After girding herself with a white apron, she went out to the back kitchen and soon reappeared carrying a pudding of noble proportions. 'Now, pass your plates,' she said, seating herself at table. 'I'm not going to tell you what's in it; you must find out,' and she stuck her knife into the rich, flaky suet crust, releasing a stream of brown gravy, and began to spoon generous helpings on to the plates.

'You could make a good meal on the smell alone,' said Charity's father, sniffing the air appreciatively. But what was that within the pudding which smelt so delicious? It was not beef, for it was cut into joints, and the joints were not those of a rabbit. Charity's parents looked puzzled. Luke was licking his lips and staring round-eyed. Then, as Mrs. Finch began cutting up Charity's portion, she exclaimed, 'Upon my soul, our Marianna, I do believe it's a fowl! Who ever heard of such extravagance!'...

If her guests had not felt hungry before, the sight and smell of the cockerel pudding had given them good appetites. In a very short time the last remnant of suet crust, with the last scraping of gravy and oddments of pork, were being spooned on to Luke's plate to accompany the last pickings of his drumstick."

—— *Still Glides the Stream*, Chapter 3

Suet-based pastry has always been a favourite in country kitchens, helping to extend scarce meat, and cooking for hours over an open fire to produce a richly succulent dish. Originally the puddings were made the size of a football, tied in a cloth and cooked in a cauldron with accompanying vegetables, but as pottery became cheaper, a large basin was used with a covering of cloth. Today it is easiest to cover the pastry lid with a piece of greaseproof paper and foil, and to put the basin into a large covered saucepan with boiling water to come half-way up the bowl. This water should be topped up with more boiling water from time to time, and the pudding will need 3-4 hours' cooking.

Cockerel Pudding

4 lb CHICKEN
8 oz BELLY PORK
1 MEDIUM ONION
1 BAY LEAF
1 TABLESPOON CHOPPED FRESH PARSLEY
SALT AND PEPPER
WATER OR CHICKEN STOCK
12 oz SELF-RAISING FLOUR
6 oz SHREDDED SUET
PINCH OF SALT

1 · Cut the chicken into eight joints.
2 · Cube the pork and chop the onion finely.
3 · Mix the flour and suet together and add salt. Mix with just enough cold water to give a soft dough. Use two-thirds of this to line a greased 2½-pint pudding basin.
4 · Put in half the pork and onion, seasoned with half the parsley, salt and pepper. Put the chicken pieces on top and add the bay leaf. Cover with remaining pork, onion, parsley and seasoning. Just cover the meat with water or stock.
5 · Roll out the remaining pastry and cover the meat. Seal the edges firmly by pressing together. Cover with a piece of greaseproof paper and foil and tie with string, leaving the covering loose enough for the suet crust to expand upwards.
6 · Put into a pan of boiling water, cover and boil gently for 4 hours, adding more boiling water to the pan from time to time to prevent burning.
7 · Serve with parsley sauce or gravy.

That splendid pudding was actually served for a Christening Tea, but there were many variations served as a main meal.

Beef and Mushroom Pudding

1 lb CHUCK STEAK
4 oz OX KIDNEY
1 oz PLAIN FLOUR
2 TEASPOONS MUSTARD POWDER
SALT AND PEPPER
8 oz MUSHROOMS
¼ PINT BEEF STOCK OR WATER
12 oz SELF-RAISING FLOUR
6 oz SHREDDED SUET
PINCH OF SALT

1 · Cut the steak into cubes. Chop the kidney into small pieces. Mix the meat with the flour, mustard, salt and pepper.
2 · Add the mushrooms cut in quarters.
3 · Mix the flour and suet together and add salt. Mix with enough cold water to give a soft dough. Use two-thirds of this to line a greased 2½-pint pudding basin.
4 · Put in the meat mixture and pour in the stock or water.
5 · Roll out the remaining pastry and cover the meat. Seal the edges firmly by pressing together. Cover with a piece of greaseproof paper and foil and tie with string, leaving the covering loose enough for the suet crust to expand upwards.
6 · Put into a pan of boiling water, cover and boil gently for 4 hours, adding more boiling water if necessary from time to time to prevent burning.

Because meat was so expensive, women and children frequently had to do without, and often made their meal from eggs, or perhaps a tiny piece of home-cured bacon, home-grown vegetables or wild food, accompanied by a lot of bread. Seasonal food was much appreciated to give variety, and gathering it was half the fun:

> "It would be school holidays then and the children at the end house always wanted to get up hours before their time. There were mushrooms in the meadows around Fordlow and they were sometimes allowed to go picking them to fry for their breakfast. More often they were not; for the dew-soaked grass was bad for their boots. 'Six shillingsworth of good shoe-leather gone for sixpen'orth of mushrooms!' their mother would cry despairingly. But some years old boots had been kept for the purpose and they would dress and creep silently downstairs, not to disturb the younger children, and with hunks of bread and butter in their hands steal out into the dewy, morning world. —— *Lark Rise*, Chapter 15

Sometimes the mushrooms were seasoned and grilled over a hot fire, or they might be simply fried in a little fat to serve with bacon. The most traditional way was to cook them gently in a little butter until just tender, and then some creamy milk was added and the mushrooms simmered for 10 minutes so that the mushrooms formed a light creamy sauce around them. Lightly seasoned and served on toast, large field mushrooms cooked this way were a delicious feast.

"Callers made a pleasant diversion in the hamlet women's day, and there were more of these than might have been expected. The first to arrive on Monday morning was old Jerry Parish with his cartload of fish and fruit. As he served some of the big houses on his round, Jerry carried quite a large stock; but the only goods he took round to the doors at Lark Rise were a box of bloaters and a basket of small sour oranges. The bloaters were sold at a penny each and the oranges at three a penny. Even at these prices they were luxuries; but, as it was still only Monday and a few coppers might remain in a few purses, the women felt at liberty to crowd round his cart to examine and criticise his wares, even if they bought nothing.

Two or three of them would be tempted to buy a bloater for their midday meal, but it had to be a soft-roed one, for, in nearly every house there were children under school age at home; so the bloater had to be shared, and the soft roes spread upon bread for the smallest ones.

'Lor' blime me!' Jerry used to say. 'Never knowed such a lot in me life for soft roes. Good job I ain't a soft-roed 'un or I should've got aten up meself before now.'"

———— *Lark Rise*, Chapter 7

The bloater is a cured herring with a strong flavour, and it is best grilled and served with a pat of butter. The herring was in huge supply in Victorian times, and very nourishing when families could afford fish. For the poorer villagers, no other fish suited their purses, although Jerry the fishmonger also carried such delicacies as John Dory. His fruit included grapes, pears and peaches as well as the sour oranges purchased by the country women in winter, which was the only season during which they were imported.

It was on Jerry's cart that tomatoes first appeared in the hamlet. They were new to Britain, flatter in shape than now, and deeply grooved and indented from the stem, probably like today's full-flavoured outdoor varieties. There were bright yellow tomatoes too, but they did not remain long on the market, and the red ones became rounder and smoother. They were commonly called 'love-apples' and treated with great suspicion – 'But you don't want any o' they – nasty sour things, they be, as only gentry can eat' was the warning from Jerry to the inquisitive little Laura in *Lark Rise*.

Bloater paste was a great favourite for teatime. Bloaters are smoked herring from the East Coast. They have a strong flavour and a slightly pinkish colour.

Bloater Paste

2 PLUMP BLOATERS
BUTTER
SALT AND PEPPER
2 oz CLARIFIED BUTTER

1 · Grill the fish until cooked through but not dry. Cool slightly and remove the skin and bones.
2 · Flake the flesh and mix with a two-thirds to equal weight of butter and with salt and pepper. Mash well and press into a serving dish.
3 · Cover with clarified butter.

Clarified Butter Melt butter very gently, and then pour into a clean dish carefully, without pouring in the milky fluid at the bottom of the saucepan, which should be discarded. Leave until firm. When this butter is melted and poured over potted meat or fish, it forms a pure, airtight seal, and this kept such food safely for a few days before refrigeration.

Spiced Herrings or Trout

6 MEDIUM HERRINGS OR TROUT
2 oz SALT
¼ oz GROUND NUTMEG
¼ oz GROUND CLOVES
¼ oz GROUND GINGER
2 BAY LEAVES
2 STRIPS LEMON PEEL
4 oz BUTTER
6 oz CLARIFIED BUTTER

1 · Wash and gut the fish and cut off the heads, tails and fins. Remove the backbones and take out the roes.
2 · Mix the salt and spices and season the fish inside and out with the mixture.
3 · Place the fish in a shallow ovenware dish and place the bay leaves and lemon peel on top. Cut the butter into flakes and dot them over the fish. Cover with foil and bake in a moderate oven (350°F/180°C/ Gas Mark 4) for 40 minutes.
4 · Cool until the fish can be handled and carefully remove skin and any bones. Break the flesh into flakes and place in a large dish or individual pots with any remaining cooking liquid.
5 · Leave until cold and then pour on melted clarified butter. Leave until firm and set. If liked, the potted fish may be kept in the refrigerator for up to 3 days.

"For other meals they depended largely on bread and butter, or, more often, bread and lard, eaten with any relish that happened to be at hand. Fresh butter was too costly for general use, but a pound was sometimes purchased in the summer, when it cost tenpence. Margarine, then called 'butterine', was already on the market, but was little used there, as most people preferred lard, especially when it was their own home-made lard flavoured with rosemary leaves. In summer there was always plenty of green food from the garden and home-made jam as long as it lasted, and sometimes an egg or two, where fowls were kept, or when eggs were plentiful and sold at twenty a shilling. —— *Lark Rise*, Chapter 1

In more affluent households, there would be leftover bits and pieces after the family and servants had eaten their fill, but all households were careful about economies in those days, and the scraps were turned into relishes to serve at breakfast or supper with bread or toast.

Potted Meat

COOKED BEEF, HAM OR POULTRY
BUTTER
SALT AND PEPPER
PINCH OF GROUND NUTMEG
CLARIFIED BUTTER

Potted meat or paste was a traditional favourite eaten on breakfast bread or toast, and it used to be made into teatime sandwiches. It is a practical way of using up oddments of meat and has far more flavour and nourishment than the commercial variety. Use one meat (such as beef) or a mixture such as beef and ham, or ham and chicken.
1 · Put the meat through the fine blade of a mincer twice, or chop very finely in a food processor.
2 · Season well to taste (adding a few drops of Worcestershire sauce or mushroom ketchup, if desired).
3 · Mix with half the meat's weight in softened butter and mash to the required consistency.
4 · Press into a serving dish and cover with clarified butter.

Potted Cheese

1 lb CHESHIRE CHEESE
3 oz UNSALTED BUTTER
1 TEASPOON MADE MUSTARD
LARGE PINCH OF GROUND MACE
PINCH OF CELERY SALT
4 oz CLARIFIED BUTTER

1 · Grate the cheese into a bowl. Add the butter, mustard, mace and celery salt.
2 · Mash together until thoroughly mixed. Press into dry jars.

3 · Cover with clarified butter. Store in a cold place.
4 · Use for flavouring cheese dishes, spreading on toast, or spooning into soups.

Potted Stilton

8 oz STILTON CHEESE
2 oz BUTTER
PINCH OF SALT
PINCH OF GROUND MACE
1 TABLESPOON PORT
2 oz CLARIFIED BUTTER

1 · Break the cheese into small pieces and mash with the butter until well blended.
2 · Season with salt and mace and work in the port.

3 · Press into small pots and cover with melted clarified butter.
4 · Leave until cold and firm.

This is a good way of using up the remains of the Christmas Stilton, and it will keep for a week or two in the refrigerator.

Workmen however enjoyed a different kind of "relish" at a mid-afternoon meal if the main hot meal was served late in the evening. On Sundays, when the meal appeared in the middle of the day, children too might partake of a rather special afternoon meal.

> "She could remember when bread and cheese and beer were at that hour taken to the forge for the men to consume standing. 'Afternoon bavour', they called it. Now a well-covered table awaited them indoors. Each man's plate was stacked with slices of bread and butter, and what was called 'a relish' was provided. 'What can we give the men for a relish at tea-time?' was an almost daily question in that household. Sometimes a blue-and-white basin of boiled new-laid eggs would be placed on the table. Three eggs per man was the standard allowance, but two or three extra were usually cooked 'in case', and at the end of the meal the basin was always empty.
> —— *Candleford Green*, Chapter 1

The Cottage Pig

"A good pig fattening in the sty promised a good winter. During its lifetime the pig was an important member of the family, and its health and condition were regularly reported in letters to children away from home, together with news of their brothers and sisters. Men callers on Sunday afternoons came, not to see the family, but the pig, and would lounge with its owner against the pigsty door for an hour, scratching piggy's back and praising his points or turning up their own noses in criticism. Ten to fifteen shillings was the price paid for a pigling when weaned, and they all delighted in getting a bargain. Some men swore by the 'dilling', as the smallest of a litter was called, saying it was little and good, and would soon catch up; others preferred to give a few shillings more for a larger young pig.

The family pig was everybody's pride and everybody's business. Mother spent hours boiling up the 'little taturs' to mash and mix with the pot-liquor, in which food had been cooked, to feed to the pig for its evening meal and help out the expensive barley meal. The children, on their way home from school, would fill their arms with sow thistle, dandelion, and choice long grass, or roam along the hedgerows on wet evenings collecting snails in a pail for the pig's supper. These piggy crunched up with great relish. 'Feyther', over and above farming out the sty, bedding down, doctoring, and so on, would even go without his nightly half-pint when, towards the end, the barley-meal bill mounted until 'it fair frightened anybody'."

—— *Lark Rise*, Chapter 1

The cottage pig was often known as "the gentleman who pays the rent" and indeed he represented the only riches of many families. He was a valuable animal because every succulent part could be used, and it was said that you could use everything "except the squeak". Hams and sides of bacon were salted down for use throughout the winter, and lard was extracted to be used for pastry and even for household ointments. Butter was rarely used, and the lard was flavoured with rosemary and spread on bread as a treat. The little bits of crisp fat left over from melting the big pieces of fat to make lard, were known as "scratchins" or "scruggins" and eaten with salt as a treat or made into cakes or pies.

Sausages were prepared, and sometimes salted or smoked for short-term preservation. Joints were eaten fresh or salted, and given to neighbours in exchange for meat when their pig was ready. Sometimes joints were given to the miller or the baker to pay for the barley-meal which had been used for fattening. Liver and other highly perishable pieces of meat were eaten at once in a celebration meal, and the trimmings were turned into faggots, pies and puddings. It was small wonder that such bounty marked a high spot in family life, and that the pig was so greatly cherished.

"Months of hard work and self-denial were brought on that night to a successful conclusion. It was a time to rejoice, and rejoice they did, with beer flowing freely and the first delicious dish of pig's fry sizzling in the frying-pan.

The next day, when the carcass had been cut up, joints of pork were distributed to those neighbours who had sent similar ones at their own pig-killing. Small plates of fry and other oddments were sent to others as a pure compliment, and no one who happened to be ill or down on his luck at these occasions was ever forgotten.

Then the housewife 'got down to it', as she said. Hams and sides of bacon were salted, to be taken out of the brine later and hung on the wall near the fireplace to dry. Lard was dried out, hog's puddings were made, and the chitterlings were cleaned and turned three days in succession under running water, according to ancient ritual. It was a busy time, but a happy one . . .

——— *Lark Rise*, Chapter 1

Pork Pudding

1½ lb LEAN PORK
12 oz PORK SAUSAGEMEAT
1 LARGE ONION
6 FRESH SAGE LEAVES
SALT AND PEPPER
12 oz SELF-RAISING FLOUR
6 oz SHREDDED SUET
¼ PINT STOCK OR WATER

1 · Cut the pork into small cubes.

2 · Form the sausagemeat into 18 small balls of equal size.

3 · Chop the onion finely.

4 · Mix the pork, sausagemeat balls, onion and sage together and season well with salt and pepper.

5 · Stir the flour and suet together and add a pinch of salt. Mix with enough cold water to make a soft dough. Use two-thirds to line a greased 2-pint pudding basin.

6 · Put in the pork mixture and sprinkle in ¼ pint water or stock. Cover with the remaining dough, sealing the edges firmly. Cover with a piece of greased greaseproof paper and then with foil and tie firmly.

7 · Put into a large pan of boiling water, cover and simmer for 4 hours, adding more boiling water to the pan occasionally to prevent burning.

Market Day Dinner

6 PORK CHOPS
2 PIG'S KIDNEYS
8 oz PIG'S LIVER
1 lb ONIONS
1 COOKING APPLE
1 TEASPOON CHOPPED FRESH SAGE
SALT AND PEPPER
1 lb POTATOES

1 · Put the chops into a greased ovenware dish. Slice the kidneys and liver and put over the chops.
2 · Slice the onions and cover the meat.
3 · Peel, core and slice the apple and arrange on top.
4 · Sprinkle on the chopped sage and season well with salt and pepper.
5 · Peel and slice the potatoes and cover the top of the dish with them.
6 · Pour on ½ pint water or stock and cover the dish.
7 · Cook in a low oven (325°F/160°C/Gas Mark 3) for 3 hours.

Bacon Roll

8 oz SELF-RAISING FLOUR
4 oz SHREDDED SUET
PINCH OF SALT
8 oz STREAKY BACON RASHERS
3 LARGE ONIONS
1 TEASPOON CHOPPED FRESH SAGE
PEPPER

1 · Mix together the flour, suet and salt, and add enough water to make a soft but firm dough. Roll out on a floured board to ½ in. thickness.
2 · Chop the bacon roughly and sprinkle half on the dough.
3 · Chop the onions finely and mix with the sage. Sprinkle on half this mixture.
4 · Top with remaining bacon and then the remaining onion mixture.
5 · Season well with pepper and a little salt, depending on the saltiness of the bacon.
6 · Roll up like a Swiss roll and wrap in greased greaseproof paper, allowing room for expansion. Wrap in foil, sealing top and edges firmly.
7 · Place in a pan half-full of boiling water, cover and boil for 3 hours, adding more water from time to time.
8 · Unwrap carefully and serve with gravy.

A variation of Bacon Roll was made when fresh liver was available, using the same recipe, but including 8 oz pig's liver, chopped very finely.

Boiled Pork and Pease Pudding

3 lb SHOULDER OF PORK
3 CARROTS
1 LARGE ONION
½ TURNIP
3 CELERY STICKS
6 PEPPERCORNS
3 SAGE LEAVES
Pease Pudding
1 lb SPLIT PEAS, SOAKED OVERNIGHT
SPRIG OF MINT
1 EGG
1 oz BUTTER
SALT AND PEPPER

As so few houses had an oven, boiled meat was frequently served, with the vegetables included in the cooking liquid. Often a boiled suet or batter pudding was put into the pan too, or a pudding made of tasty and nourishing pulses.

1 · Put the shoulder of pork into a large pan and cover with cold water. Cover the pan and bring to the boil. Skim and boil for 15 minutes.

2 · Cut the carrots in quarters and slice the onion, turnip and celery. Add to the pan with the peppercorns and sage. Cover and boil gently for 1½ hours.

3 · To make the pudding, tie the soaked peas and mint in a piece of clean cloth, allowing room for the peas to swell. Put this into the pan with the pork and boil for 1 hour.

4 · Undo the cloth carefully, and sieve the peas.

5 · Mix with beaten egg, butter and plenty of seasoning.

6 · Put into a clean piece of cloth and boil with the pork for 30 minutes.

7 · Serve with the pork, vegetables and gravy made from the cooking liquid.

Pork and Kidney Pie

1 lb PORK SHOULDER
3 PIG'S KIDNEYS
2 TEASPOONS CHOPPED FRESH SAGE OR BASIL
PINCH OF GROUND NUTMEG
PINCH OF SALT
2 MEDIUM CARROTS
1 MEDIUM ONION
½ PINT STOCK
8 oz SHORTCRUST PASTRY

1 · Cut the pork and kidneys into small pieces and put into a pie dish.

2 · Add the herbs, nutmeg, salt and pepper.

3 · Chop the carrots and onion coarsely and sprinkle on the meat.

4 · Mix well and pour in the stock.

5 · Cover with a piece of foil and cook in a low oven (325°F/160°C/Gas Mark 3) for 1 hour.

6 · Remove the foil and leave the meat to cool for 30 minutes.

7 · Cover with pastry and bake in a hot oven (400°F/200°C/Gas Mark 6) for 30 minutes until the pastry is golden brown.

Raised Pork Pie

5 oz LARD
½ PINT WATER
1 lb PLAIN FLOUR
½ TEASPOON SALT
1¼ lb SHOULDER PORK
½ TEASPOON CHOPPED FRESH SAGE
SALT AND PEPPER
2 PIG'S TROTTERS OR 1 lb PORK BONES
1 PINT WATER
EGG FOR GLAZING

Traditionally the pastry for raised pies is made with hot water, and the very soft paste is moulded with the hands over a wooden mould. Housewives without a mould used a jam jar, but today it is easier to make the pie in a tin with a removable base.

1 · Put the lard and water into a pan and bring to the boil.

2 · Tip in the flour all at once, and the salt.

3 · Take the pan off the heat and work to a smooth, stiff paste until there are no cracks in the dough.

4 · Cover with a cloth and leave in a warm place for 30 minutes.

5 · When the pastry is just warm, knead again and mould two-thirds over a jam jar, or inside a 6-in. cake tin.

6 · Dice the meat and mix with sage and seasoning.

7 · Fill the pastry case and cover with remaining pastry, sealing the edges.

8 · Make a small round hole in the lid, filling it with a ball of pastry or foil. Brush the top of the pie with a little egg beaten with a pinch of salt.

9 · If made without a tin, tie a double thickness of greaseproof paper or foil firmly round the pastry to keep it in a good shape.

10 · Bake in a moderate oven (350°C/180°F/Gas Mark 4) for 2 hours, and leave until cold before removing paper or foil, or taking from the tin.

11 · While the pie is cooking, simmer the trotters or bones in the water for 1½ hours.

12 · Remove the bones and leave the stock until cold.

13 · When the pie is cold, remove the "plug" from the lid, and spoon in the cold stock a little at a time so that the meat absorbs the liquid which will form a jelly.

14 · Leave for 12 hours or until firm before removing from the foil or tin.

"Another cooking process Laura was never to see elsewhere and which perhaps may have been peculiar to smithy families was known as 'salamandering'. For this thin slices of bacon or ham were spread out on a large plate and taken to the smithy, where the plate was placed on the anvil. The smith then heated red-hot one end of a large, flat iron utensil known as the 'salamander' and held it above the plate until the rashers were crisp and curled. Shelled boiled, or poached, eggs were eaten with this dish."

———— Candleford Green, Chapter 3

Bacon was always popular, with the salted joints and sides hanging in the kitchen to be sliced as needed. Rashers with eggs were eaten at any meal, and streaky rashers were used in puddings and pies. Fat boiled bacon was eaten for breakfast and in sandwiches. A kind of bacon omelette called a "fraze" was a very old dish which was much enjoyed.

Bacon Fraze

8 EGGS
3 TABLESPOONS SINGLE CREAM OR TOP OF THE MILK
1 oz PLAIN FLOUR
8 oz THIN BACON RASHERS

1 · Beat the eggs and cream with the flour to make a batter.
2 · Fry or grill the bacon crisply and drain well.
3 · Put half the butter into a lightly greased frying pan and cook gently.

4 · When just set, arrange the bacon rashers on top and cover with remaining batter.
5 · When set, turn carefully and brown the other side.
6 · Serve with mustard.

Boiled Bacon with Parsley Sauce

4 lb BACON JOINT
1 BAY LEAF
6 PEPPERCORNS
1 TABLESPOON LIGHT SOFT BROWN SUGAR
Sauce
2 oz BUTTER
2 oz PLAIN FLOUR
½ PINT MILK
½ PINT BACON STOCK
SALT AND PEPPER
2 TABLESPOONS CHOPPED FRESH PARSLEY

1 · Soak the bacon joint for 4 hours.

2 · Drain well and put into a large pan. Cover with cold water and add the bay leaf, peppercorns and sugar. Bring to the boil and reduce heat. Simmer for 2 hours.

3 · Drain the bacon and strip off the skin. Return to the cooking liquid to keep warm.

4 · To make the sauce, melt the butter and stir in the flour gradually, off the heat, until the mixture is smooth. Work in the milk and stock gradually, stirring until smooth. Cook over low heat, stirring well, until smooth and creamy. Season and add the parsley.

5 · Serve the bacon in thick slices with the parsley sauce. Traditionally this was always eaten with broad beans.

"Indoors, the kitchen table was laid with pies and tarts and custards and, in the place of honour at the head of the table, the dish of the evening, a stuffed collar chine of bacon.

. . .

For the stuffed chine the largest dish in the house had to be used. It was a great round joint, being the whole neck of a pig, cut and cured specially for the hay-home supper. It was lavishly stuffed with sage and onions and was altogether very rich and highly-flavoured. It would not have suited modern digestions, but most of those present at the hay-home supper ate of it largely and enjoyed it." —— *Candleford Green*, Chapter 4

Sage and onion was a popular stuffing for this piece of salted pork, but a more delicate mixture of herbs is preferred by "modern digestions".

Stuffed Chine

1 CHINE OF SALT PORK
PARSLEY
SPRING ONIONS
THYME
MARJORAM

1 · The chine of meat is cut between the shoulder blades across the backbone in a square shape. Stand the meat on end on a flat surface.

2 · Slash through the meat to the bone 5-6 times. Turn the meat and do the same with the other side.

3 · Soak in cold water for 24 hours.

4 · Take a large quantity of parsley with a little of the other herbs – sometimes lettuce is included, and raspberry leaves. Chop the herbs very finely and use them to fill the slashes made in the meat.

5 · Tie firmly in a piece of cloth and put into a pan of cold water. Cover and simmer for 4 hours, changing the water once.

6 · Cool in the cooking liquid for 3 hours, drain and leave in the cloth.

7 · Press under a weight.

8 · Unwrap and slice thickly from the fat end, parallel to the fat, so that the slices consist of pink and white meat striped with green herbs.

9 · Serve with vinegar.

Sausage-making was part of every country housewife's duty when the family pig was killed. They were made to personal requirements, either ground finely or coarsely; with a mixture of meat; with or without bread or rusk; and with a huge range of flavourings. Sausages are easy to make and today may be stored in a freezer. The mixture should be about two-thirds lean pork to one-third fat. Shoulder pork gives a good mixture of fat and lean, but belly pork is cheaper. Some people like to add a little salted pork or bacon which gives a light pink colour.

Breadcrumbs, either fresh or dried, are usually added to give firmness and bulk to the meat. A little water added to the mixture makes the sausages easier to fill into skins, but tomato or apple purée may be added for a flavoured sausage. Sage, thyme, marjoram, basil and pennyroyal are all suitable herbs to flavour the meat, and some people like a touch of garlic. Freshly ground black pepper, sea salt and a pinch of nutmeg are also essential seasonings, and other spices may be added as desired.

The ingredients should be minced coarsely or finely, or may be prepared to the required fineness in a food processor. For a simple sausage if skins cannot be obtained, the meat mixture may be wrapped in caul fat which is sometimes known as "veil". This is like a thin transparent skin with a veined pattern of fat, and it may be bought or ordered from many butchers (pork butchers usually have a ready supply). This fatty skin should be soaked in tepid water, allowing 1 tablespoon vinegar to 2 pints water. When the fat is soft and pliable, it may be cut into squares with scissors and wrapped round flat patties of meat with a sage leaf tucked under the skin for appearance and flavour. This gives a firm casing for the meat which melts slightly during cooking and shows an attractive veining.

When the ingredients have been prepared and mixed by chopping or mincing, a filling nozzle has to be fitted to the mincer. The end of the skin should be lifted from the bowl where it is soaking and pushed well on to the nozzle. The skin should be shirred on to the nozzle, but not overlaid on itself, and the other end left an inch or two below the end of the nozzle. The mincer is then started and as the meat comes through it is possible to control the filling of the skin firmly by regulating the slip-off nozzle end with the fingers (it is a great help to have a second pair of hands during this operation). The weight of the sausage is considerable as it leaves the filler, and it should be loaded carefully on to a tray or other clean surface. The length of the sausage may run straight, or be coiled round, or twisted into convenient lengths.

Air which accumulates in the skins should be pressed out as the meat runs in. If using synthetic casings, it is important to have dry hands, free from grease, or the skins will not fill evenly, and will be under-stuffed. If they are filled too tightly they will burst when cooked.

Simple Sausages

1 lb LEAN PORK
8 oz PORK FAT
1 TEASPOON SALT
½ TEASPOON GROUND ALLSPICE
PINCH OF BLACK PEPPER
PINCH OF DRIED MARJORAM
1 oz DRIED WHITE BREADCRUMBS

1 · Mince the lean pork and pork fat twice, or chop finely in a food processor.
2 · Mix together well and season together.

3 · Stir in the breadcrumbs. Fill the mixture into skins or form into small round cakes.

Spiced Sausages

12 oz DRY WHITE BREAD
2 lb LEAN PORK
12 oz PORK FAT
¾ oz SALT
¼ oz GROUND BLACK PEPPER
¼ oz GROUND GINGER
¼ oz GROUND MACE

1 · Soak the bread in cold water. Then squeeze out the moisture with the hands.
2 · Put the lean pork and fat through the coarse blade of a mincer, or chop coarsely

with a food processor.
3 · Mix with the bread and seasonings and then mince or chop finely.
4 · Fill into skins or form into small cakes.

Cottage Sausages

1 lb SHOULDER PORK
4 oz BREADCRUMBS
SALT AND PEPPER
PINCH OF SAGE OR MARJORAM

1 · The best pork to use is half fat and half lean. Put through a mincer, or chop finely in a food processor.
2 · Soak the breadcrumbs in cold water, then squeeze them almost dry.
3 · Mix well with the meat, seasoning well and adding herbs as liked. Leave to stand in

a cold place for 3-4 hours.
4 · Either fill sausage skins with a hand-filler, or with an attachment on an electric mincer. If preferred, form into patty shapes, which may be covered with pieces of caul skin (veiling), if available.
5 · Use within 24 hours.

Herb Sausages

2 lb SHOULDER PORK
2 TEASPOONS SALT
4 TEASPOONS DRIED SAGE
2 TEASPOONS DRIED MARJORAM
½-1 TEASPOON GARLIC POWDER
¼ TEASPOON GROUND CLOVES
¼ TEASPOON GROUND BLACK PEPPER
PINCH OF CAYENNE PEPPER

The flavour of these sausages is very special and it is worth using good meat for them. The shoulder meat gives a good mixture of fat and lean.

1 · Mince or chop the meat finely and work in all the seasonings.
2 · Mince or chop again.
3 · Chill for 24 hours so that the flavour matures.
4 · Fill into skins or form into small cakes.

Pork Patties

12 oz SALT BELLY PORK
1 lb PIG'S LIVER
PEPPER
NUTMEG
SAGE LEAVES
CAUL SKIN

1 · Weigh the salt pork when it has been skinned and boned to get the correct weight. Either mince the liver and pork coarsely, or chop in a food processor (the mixture should not be smooth).
2 · Season well with pepper and nutmeg.
3 · Take 2 oz quantities of the mixture and shape into thick, flat patties.
4 · Put a sage leaf on each one and wrap in a piece of caul skin with the join underneath.
5 · Place the patties close together in a shallow ovenware dish and cover with foil. Bake in a low oven (325°F/160°C/Gas Mark 3) for 1 hour.
6 · Eat hot or cold.

If caul fat is not available, the patties may be made without it, but the meat must be very firmly pressed together, and the patties placed close together for cooking.

When all the main dishes had been prepared, there were always all sorts of bits and pieces of meat and offal to be turned into dishes which were usually eaten at the teatime meal around five o'clock at the end of the working day, which was the main meal for most families. Such dishes as faggots and brawn were prepared at home, along with a variety of meat loaves which today we might call pâtés.

Faggots

1½ lb PIG'S LIVER
6 oz BACON
2 MEDIUM ONIONS
7 oz FRESH WHITE BREADCRUMBS
3 oz SHREDDED SUET
2 TEASPOONS CHOPPED FRESH SAGE
1 TEASPOON CHOPPED FRESH BASIL
SALT AND PEPPER

1 · Mince the liver, bacon and onions together and mix with the other ingredients.
2 · Form into 8 balls and roll them in a little flour.
3 · Pack closely together in a baking tin and bake in a moderate oven (350°F/ 180°C/Gas Mark 4) for 30 minutes.
4 · Serve with rich gravy.

Pork Brawn

1 SALT PORK HOCK WITH TROTTER
PEPPER
6 FRESH SAGE LEAVES, FINELY CHOPPED

Brawn was usually made to use up the head of the animal, but this simple version is more easily prepared.

1 · Put the meat into a pan and just cover with water. Cover the pan and simmer for 1½ hours.
2 · Lift the meat from the bones and cut into small pieces.
3 · Season lightly with pepper and sage.
4 · Put the bones back into the liquid and simmer until the liquid is reduced to half.
5 · Strain over the meat, stir well and put into bowls. When cool and just setting, stir again and leave to set.
6 · Serve with vinegar and mustard.

For a richer flavour, cook the meat with 1 crushed garlic clove, 1 bay leaf and 1 thyme sprig, removing the herbs before shredding the meat.

Farmwife's Pork Loaf

3 RASHERS STREAKY BACON
4 oz SMALL MUSHROOMS
1 oz BUTTER
1 TABLESPOON OIL
1 MEDIUM ONION
3 oz CHICKEN LIVERS
1 lb PORK SAUSAGEMEAT
SALT AND PEPPER
½ TEASPOON MIXED FRESH HERBS
4 oz FRESH BREADCRUMBS
2 EGGS
2 BAY LEAVES

1 · Derind the bacon and stretch the rashers with a broad-bladed knife.

2 · Grease a 1 lb loaf tin or casserole and arrange the rashers across the bottom and up the sides, leaving a gap between each rasher.

3 · Slice 8 mushrooms thinly and arrange between the rashers.

4 · Heat the butter and oil together and fry the finely chopped onion until soft and golden. Lift out onion and set aside.

5 · Fry the chicken livers lightly and chop roughly.

6 · Chop the remaining mushrooms and fry in the fat for 3 minutes.

7 · Put the sausagemeat into a bowl and work in the onion, chicken livers and mushrooms and any pan juices.

8 · Season well and add the breadcrumbs, herbs and eggs. Put into the prepared tin and fold over the bacon rashers. Place the bay leaves on top.

9 · Cover with a piece of foil, and stand the tin in a roasting tin containing about 1 in. water. Bake in a moderate oven (325°F/160°C/Gas Mark 3) for 1½ hours.

10 · Press under weights for 24 hours.

11 · Remove bay leaves and turn the loaf out on to serving dish.

12 · Serve with toast or salad.

Simple Pork Loaf

12 oz PIG'S LIVER
2 lb BELLY PORK
1 LARGE ONION, CHOPPED
1 LARGE EGG
1 TABLESPOON PLAIN FLOUR
1 TABLESPOON CHOPPED FRESH PARSLEY
SALT, PEPPER AND NUTMEG
8 oz STREAKY BACON RASHERS

1 · Put liver and pork through the coarse screen of a mincer, or chop them finely in a food processor.

2 · Soften the onion in a little butter.

3 · Put the meat mixture, onion and cooking juices, egg, flour, parsley and seasonings into a food processor or blender and blend for 5 seconds.

4 · Remove the rind from the bacon rashers, and flatten the rashers with a knife so that they are very thin.

5 · Line a casserole or terrine with the bacon rashers.

6 · Put in the mixture and fold over the ends of the bacon.

7 · Cover with a piece of greaseproof paper and a lid. Put the container in a roasting tin of water and cook in a moderate oven (350°F/180°C/Gas Mark 4) for 1½ hours.

8 · Remove from roasting tin and cool for 24 hours under heavy weights.

9 · Turn out before slicing.

Bacon Loaf

12 oz UNSMOKED BACK BACON RASHERS
1 lb LEAN PORK OR VEAL
1 SMALL ONION
6 oz FRESH WHOLEMEAL BREADCRUMBS
2 EGGS
SALT AND PEPPER
PINCH OF GROUND NUTMEG

1 · Remove rinds from 4 bacon rashers and press out the bacon thinly with a knife.

2 · Line a loaf tin with these rashers. Reserve 4 more rashers.

3 · Mince the remaining bacon with pork or veal and onion. Mix with breadcrumbs, eggs, salt, pepper and nutmeg.

4 · Take the remaining bacon and remove rinds. Press out rashers thinly and cut them in half.

5 · Put one-third bacon mixture into the tin and top with four pieces of bacon. Add another layer of bacon mixture and the four remaining bacon pieces. Top with another layer of bacon mixture.

6 · Cover with foil and put the loaf tin into a roasting tin containing 1 in. hot water. Bake in a moderate oven (325°F/160°C/Gas Mark 3) for 1½ hours.

7 · Remove from oven and put under heavy weights until cold.

8 · Serve in thick slices with salad.

Puddings and Cakes

"When King Arthur first did reign,
    He rul-ed like a king;
He bought three sacks of barley meal
    To make a plum pud-ding.

The pudding it was made
    And duly stuffed with plums,
And lumps of suet put in it
    As big as my two thumbs.

The king and queen sat down to it
    And all the lords beside;
And what they couldn't eat that night
    The queen next morning fried.

Every time Laura heard this sung she saw the queen, a gold crown on her head, her train over her arm, and her sleeves rolled up, holding the frying-pan over the fire. Of course, a queen *would* have fried pudding for breakfast: ordinary common people seldom had any left over to fry."

—— *Lark Rise*, Chapter 4

Indeed the "ordinary common people" never had anything left over, and every item of food was precious. When any ingredient was free, full advantage was taken, with the women spending many hours gathering or gleaning ears of wheat to make the winter supply of flour.

"Bread had to be bought, and that was a heavy item, with so many growing children to be fed; but flour for the daily pudding and an occasional plain cake could be laid in for the winter without any cash outlay. After the harvest had been carried from the fields, the women and children swarmed over the stubble picking up the ears of wheat the horse-rake had missed."

—— *Lark Rise*, Chapter 1

In *Lark Rise*, there is a description of this domestic harvest which went on for as long as three weeks from "daybreak until nightfall, with only two short breaks for refreshment". A woman would take four or five children to bind the single ears together, then carry them home on their heads each night. The corn was threshed at home and sent to the miller to be made into flour, payment being made by the miller taking a percentage of the flour. The sack of meal was often displayed on a chair in the living room and passers-by were invited to inspect the result of a family's hard labour.

Naturally, flour played a large part in everyday cooking. Sweet floury puddings quelled appetites and also gave energy. Roly-polys were particularly useful since they were cooked in a pot alongside the savoury part of the meal and the vegetables, as they had been cooked for centuries over an open fire.

Jam Roly-Poly

6 oz SELF-RAISING FLOUR
PINCH OF SALT
3 oz SHREDDED SUET
¼ PINT COLD WATER
8 oz PLUM OR BLACKCURRANT JAM

1 · Stir together the flour, salt and suet. Mix with the water to form a firm dough.
2 · Roll out to a rectangle 8×12 in. and spread thickly with jam.
3 · Roll up firmly and wrap lightly in a piece of greased greaseproof paper. Wrap in foil, sealing the top and ends firmly.
4 · Put the roly-poly into a large saucepan of boiling water and cover. Boil gently for 2 hours, adding a little more boiling water if necessary. (If preferred, you can place the roly-poly on a greased baking sheet, and bake in a hot oven (425°F/220°C/Gas Mark 7) for 40 minutes.)
5 · Unroll very carefully and serve hot.

Spotted Dog

8 oz SELF-RAISING FLOUR
PINCH OF SALT
4 oz SHREDDED SUET
1 oz SUGAR
8 oz CURRANTS
¼ PINT COLD WATER

1 · Mix together the flour, salt, suet, sugar and currants and mix to a firm dough with the water.

2 · Form into a cylinder about 8 in. long and wrap in greased greaseproof paper and then in foil, sealing the edges firmly but leaving room for expansion.

3 · Put into a pan of boiling water and cover. Boil gently for 2 hours, adding a little more boiling water if necessary.

4 · Unroll carefully and serve hot with brown sugar and butter.

"The children at the end house loved fetching in the palm and putting it in pots and vases and hanging it over the picture frames. Better still, they loved the old custom of eating figs on Palm Sunday. The week before, the innkeeper's wife would get in a stock to be sold in pennyworths in her small grocery store. Some of the more expert cooks among the women would use these to make fig puddings for dinner and the children bought pennyworths and ate them out of screws of blue sugar paper on their way to Sunday school.

The gathering of the palm branches must have been a survival from old Catholic days, when, in many English churches, the willow served for palm to be blessed on Palm Sunday. The original significance of eating figs on that day had long been forgotten; but it was regarded as an important duty, and children ordinarily selfish would give one of their figs, or at least a bite out of one, to the few unfortunates who had been given no penny."

—— *Lark Rise*, Chapter 15

Figgy Pudding

8 oz DRIED FIGS
1 LEMON
4 oz WHOLEMEAL BREADCRUMBS
4 oz SHREDDED SUET
4 oz PLAIN FLOUR
1 TEASPOON BAKING POWDER
1 TEASPOON GROUND MIXED SPICE
3 oz DARK SOFT BROWN SUGAR
2 EGGS
2 TABLESPOONS MILK

1 · Chop the figs into small pieces and put into a bowl together with the grated lemon rind and juice.

2 · In another bowl, mix the breadcrumbs, suet, flour, baking powder, spice and sugar.

3 · Stir in the figs and lemon juice and then beat in the eggs and milk.

4 · Put into a well-greased pudding bowl and cover with a piece of greased grease-proof paper and then a piece of foil. Tie firmly, leaving room for expansion.

5 · Put into a pan with boiling water to come half-way up the pudding basin. Cover and boil gently for 3 hours, adding more boiling water from time to time so that the pan does not boil dry.

6 · Turn out and serve with custard.

"Christmas Day passed very quietly. The men had a holiday from work and the children from school and the churchgoers attended special Christmas services. Mothers who had young children would buy them an orange each and a handful of nuts; but, except at the end house and the inn, there was no hanging up of stockings, and those who had no kind elder sister or aunt in service to send them parcels got no Christmas presents.

Still, they did manage to make a little festival of it. Every year the farmer killed an ox for the purpose and gave each of his men a joint of beef, which duly appeared on the Christmas dinner-table together with plum pudding – not Christmas pudding, but suet duff with a good sprinkling of raisins."

——— *Lark Rise*, Chapter 15

Plum Duff for Christmas

6 oz SELF-RAISING FLOUR
3 oz SHREDDED SUET
4 oz CURRANTS
4 oz STONED RAISINS
4 oz DEMERARA SUGAR
PINCH OF GROUND MIXED SPICE
¼ PINT MILK

1 · Stir together the flour, suet, dried fruit, sugar and spice and mix with the milk to make a stiff dough.
2 · Wrap loosely in greased greaseproof paper and then in foil, sealing the edges firmly but leaving room for expansion.

3 · Put into a pan of boiling water, cover and boil gently for 2 hours, adding more boiling water if necessary so that the pan does not burn dry.
4 · Unroll carefully and serve with a jug of custard.

Another version of the Christmas Pudding was the fruited dumpling, that was eaten with the juices from the roast beef. These dumplings were originally enclosed in pieces of netting, but they are now more easily wrapped in small pieces of cloth.

Poor Man's Christmas Pudding

4 oz SHREDDED SUET
3 oz DRY WHITE BREADCRUMBS
4 oz CURRANTS
1 oz CHOPPED MIXED CANDIED PEEL
PINCH OF GROUND CINNAMON
1 oz LIGHT SOFT BROWN SUGAR
1 EGG AND 1 EGG YOLK

1 · Mix all the ingredients together to form a very stiff dough.
2 · Divide the mixture into quarters and form each portion into a ball.
3 · Cut four 8 inch squares of clean white cloth and grease them lightly.
4 · Put a ball of dough on each one and tie firmly, allowing room for expansion.
5 · Put into a pan of boiling water, cover and boil for 1 hour.
6 · Unwrap carefully and serve with a jug of custard.

"The apples would not be fit to eat, for the tree was an annual souring. Jake had favoured that apple because it was a good keeper, and had had several trees of that kind in his garden. Every year about Candlemas time he had gone round the village with a basketful of the fruit and handed out one apple for each member of the family at the doors of those who had shown him small kindnesses. 'Mind you bakes 'em well, missis, and you'll find they'll come up as white and as light as snow, and when 'em be done, you mas up the inners wi' a knob o' fresh butter and all the brown sugar you've got in the pantry, then you'll know why Eve stole the apple,' he would say." —— *Still Glides the Stream*, Chapter 1

Jake's way with an apple is delicious in the dark winter months after Christmas when big Bramley Seedlings are available, whose flesh breaks into a soft pulp. Apples were always popular because they kept right through the year and could be used in the popular suet puddings and also in batter puddings. Originally the batter of eggs, milk and flour had been poured over fruit in a basin and then boiled, but as the oven began to be used more often, crisply baked fruit batters became a great treat.

Baked Apple Batter

1 lb EATING APPLES
PINCH OF GROUND CINNAMON
1 oz BUTTER
2 oz LIGHT SOFT BROWN SUGAR
3 EGGS
5 oz SELF-RAISING FLOUR
4 TABLESPOONS MILK

If liked, chopped rhubarb may be used instead, and then ginger is a better spice to use than cinnamon.

1 · Grease an ovenware dish and put in the apples which have been peeled, cored and chopped roughly.
2 · Sprinkle with spice and sugar and dot with flakes of butter.
3 · Beat the eggs, flour and milk to a thick cream and pour over the fruit.
4 · Bake in a hot oven (425°F/220°C/Gas Mark 7) for 35 minutes.
5 · Serve hot with butter and brown sugar, or with cream.

Soft Fruit Saucer Batters

2 oz SOFT FRUIT
3 oz CASTER SUGAR
1 EGG
3 oz SELF-RAISING FLOUR
7 fl oz MILK

These more delicate "batters" were made from oddments of soft fruit from cottage gardens, such as raspberries, blackcurrants or gooseberries, or with blackberries from the hedgerows. It was usual to bake batters or pies in large old saucers, but if these are not available, individual large Yorkshire Pudding tins may be used.

1 · Mix the fruit and sugar and put into a covered ovenware dish.

2 · Bake in a moderately hot oven (400°F/200°C/Gas Mark 6) while the batters are cooking.

3 · To prepare these, whisk the egg yolk, flour and milk to make a creamy batter. Whisk the egg whites to stiff peaks and fold into the batter.

4 · Grease 6 large saucers and divide the batter between them.

5 · Put the dish of fruit on the lowest shelf of the oven, and the saucers in the centre. Bake for 20 minutes.

6 · Put three of the batters on to a warm serving dish and spoon on the hot fruit. Quickly cover with the remaining batters and sprinkle with sugar before serving.

"Milk was a rare luxury, as it had to be fetched a mile and a half from the farmhouse. The cost was not great: a penny a jug or can, irrespective of size. It was, of course, skimmed milk, but hand-skimmed, not separated, and so still had some small proportion of cream left. A few families fetched it daily; but many did not bother about it. The women said they preferred their tea neat, and it did not seem to occur to them that the children needed milk. Many of them never tasted it from the time they were weaned until they went out in the world. Yet they were stout-limbed and rosy-cheeked and full of life and mischief.

The skimmed milk was supposed by the farmer to be sold at a penny a pint, that remaining unsold going to feed his own calves and pigs. But the dairymaid did not trouble to measure it; she just filled the proffered vessel and let it go as 'a pen'orth'. Of course, the jugs and cans got larger and larger. One old woman increased the size of her vessels by degrees until she had the impudence to take a small, new, tin cooking boiler which was filled without question."

—— *Lark Rise*, Chapter 1

Some people did make rice puddings because such a pudding was considered to be soothing and strengthening, and the children of the village could buy spoonfuls of rice pudding and prunes from one of the old ladies who made sweetmeats. The more delicate milk puddings such as custards were reserved for invalids ("for the sick there were custard puddings, home-made jellies and half-bottles of port").

Cottage Rice Pudding

2½ oz ROUND PUDDING RICE
2 PINTS CREAMY MILK
2 oz SUGAR
1 oz BUTTER
PINCH OF GROUND NUTMEG

When butter was scarce, a piece of suet was put in for extra nourishment, and sometimes an egg was beaten in half-way through cooking.

1 · Put the rice and half the milk into a piedish and stir in the sugar and butter.
2 · Cook in a low oven (275°F/140°C/Gas Mark 1) for 1 hour.
3 · Stir in the remaining milk and continue cooking for 1 hour. Stir again and sprinkle with nutmeg and continue cooking for 1 hour. This long slow cooking is the secret of a successful and creamy rice pudding.

Candleford Custard

1 PINT SINGLE CREAM OR CREAMY MILK
1 VANILLA POD
3 EGGS
2 oz SUGAR
PINCH OF GROUND NUTMEG

1 · Put the cream into a pan with the vanilla pod. Heat until the liquid is just under boiling point.
2 · Beat the eggs lightly with the sugar.
3 · Remove the vanilla pod from the pan and pour the warm liquid on to the eggs. Whisk thoroughly and strain into a buttered piedish or straight-sided ovenware dish.
4 · Stand the dish in a roasting tin of water. Sprinkle the surface of the custard with nutmeg.
5 · Bake in a low oven (325°F/160°C/Gas Mark 3) for 1 hour.
6 · Serve the custard warm or cold.

Port Wine Jelly

1 PINT PORT
4 oz CASTER SUGAR
1 oz GELATINE
¼ PINT WATER
1 TEASPOON LEMON JUICE
PINCH OF GROUND CINNAMON
PINCH OF GROUND NUTMEG

1 · Put half the port into a pan with the sugar and heat gently until the sugar has dissolved.
2 · Put the water into a cup and sprinkle on the gelatine. Stand the cup in a pan of hot water and stir gently over low heat until the gelatine is very syrupy.
3 · Stir into the hot port and add the lemon juice and spices.
4 · Strain into a bowl or mould and stir in the remaining port. Leave until set.
5 · Serve with sweet biscuits.

Few families could afford such luxuries and the nearest that they got to a celebration "pudding" was a cheesecake which might be served at one of the special Feasts, or at teatime. The traditional version was made with soft cheese, but sometimes the filling was "lemon cheese" which we know today as lemon curd.

Feasting Cheesecake

8 oz SHORTCRUST PASTRY
12 oz SOFT CURD CHEESE
2 oz SOFTENED BUTTER
3 oz CASTER SUGAR
2 EGGS
2 TABLESPOONS SINGLE CREAM
1 TABLESPOON BRANDY
PINCH OF GROUND MIXED SPICE
2 oz STONED RAISINS OR CURRANTS

1 · Line an 8 in. greased flan tin with the pastry.
2 · Prick with a fork and bake in a moderate oven (350°F/180°C/Gas Mark 4) for 20 minutes. Leave to cool.
3 · Beat the cheese with the butter, sugar, eggs, cream, brandy and spice until smooth. Stir in the raisins or currants.
4 · Put into the pastry case and bake in a moderate oven (325°F/160°C/Gas Mark 3) for 40 minutes.
5 · Serve cold.

If liked, individual cheesecakes may be prepared, and the pastry cases need only be baked for 10 minutes, and the little cheesecakes for 25 minutes.

Rather oddly, fruit tarts which we might consider to be everyday fare were considered great treats, and are only mentioned in connection with well-to-do households where they were served with thick cream. Gooseberry and rhubarb tarts were only mentioned by Flora Thompson on two special occasions in Laura's life.

Fruit Tart

8 oz SHORTCRUST PASTRY
1 lb GOOSEBERRIES, RHUBARB OR PLUMS
6 oz SUGAR
PINCH OF GROUND CINNAMON OR GINGER

1 · Roll out the pastry and line a 7 in. tin.
2 · Top and tail gooseberries, chop rhubarb or halve plums and fill the pastry case.
3 · Sprinkle with the sugar and spice.

4 · Bake in a moderate oven (375°F/190°C/Gas Mark 5) for 40 minutes.
5 · Serve hot or cold, sprinkled with a little extra sugar.

"'Have a potato cake? I found young Biddy had laid an egg this morning, her first and not very big, so I thought I'd make us a cake for tea of those cold potatoes in the pantry. A bit of sugar can always be spared. That's cheap enough.'

Laura ate the cake with great relish, for it was delicious, straight from the oven, and it was also a mark of her mother's favour; the little ones were not allowed to eat between meals. . . .

Her mother's pastry board and rolling-pin still stood on a white cloth on one end of the table, and the stew for dinner, mostly composed of vegetables, but very savoury-smelling, simmered upon the hob. She had a sudden impulse to tell mother how much she loved her; but in the early 'teens such feelings cannot be put into words, and all she could do was to praise the potato cake."

—— *Over to Candleford*, Chapter 14

Cakes and sweet things have always been a sign of family love, showing the special affection which mothers have for their husbands and children. A child singled out to have a "taster", as Laura called her sample snack, would feel very special indeed as the recipient of her mother's individual attention and confidences.

A hundred years ago, elaborate cakes were rare, and certainly never made at home. A woman would use a flat iron plate or "griddle" over an open fire, or would bake in the wood- or coal-fired oven, and cake mixtures were simple to suit the budget and the difficult and variable cooking temperatures. Pancakes, scones and potato cakes were quickly made from simple ingredients in the store cupboard, and were ready hot and welcoming when children returned after walking three or four miles home from school.

Potato Cakes

8 oz POTATOES
1 oz BUTTER
½ oz SUGAR
1 EGG
4 oz PLAIN FLOUR
½ TEASPOON BAKING POWDER
¼ TEASPOON SALT

1 · Peel the potatoes and boil them until tender. Drain very well and shake the potatoes for a minute or two over low heat to drive off excess moisture.
2 · Mash well, working in the butter, sugar and egg.
3 · Sieve the flour, baking powder and salt, and work into the potatoes. Knead well to make a soft pliable dough.
4 · Roll out ½ in. thick on a lightly floured surface. Cut into 3 in. rounds and put on a lightly greased baking sheet. Prick lightly with a fork.
5 · Bake in a hot oven (425°F/220°C/Gas Mark 7) for 10 minutes.
6 · Serve hot with butter.

If preferred, the potato scones may be cooked in the original manner on a griddle. Grease a griddle or thick frying-pan lightly, and cook the scones for 5 minutes each side, turning them carefully half-way through cooking.

Drop Scones

8 oz SELF-RAISING FLOUR
1 oz CASTER SUGAR
1 TEASPOON CREAM OF TARTAR
2 EGGS
½ PINT MILK

1 · Sieve the flour into a bowl and stir in the sugar and cream of tartar.
2 · Beat the eggs and milk together and beat into the flour to make a thick batter.
3 · Grease a griddle or thick frying-pan lightly and warm to moderate heat.
4 · Pour on tablespoons of batter, a little way apart, and cook until bubbles form and burst on the surface of the batter.
5 · Turn carefully and cook on other sides until golden brown.
6 · Lift scones on to a wire rack and wrap in a clean cloth while warm so that they remain soft.
7 · Eat the scones freshly made with butter and honey.

Griddle Scones

8 oz SELF-RAISING FLOUR
¼ TEASPOON SALT
1½ oz BUTTER
1 oz SUGAR
¼ PINT MILK

1 · Sieve the flour and salt together and rub in the butter until the mixture is like fine breadcrumbs.
2 · Stir in the sugar and mix with the milk to make a soft but firm dough.
3 · Knead well and roll out ½ in. thick.

Cut into 2 in. rounds.
4 · Sprinkle a hot griddle or thick frying-pan with flour and place the scones on top.
5 · Cook until golden brown underneath. Turn carefully and cook until the other sides are golden brown.

The whole family enjoyed such simple treats, and even at the Flower Show expected nothing more than "whiffs of hot tea steam and a tempting aroma of spiced dough cake". Baking powder and self-raising flour were only produced commercially in the 1880s and the latter was not widely used until the 1920s, and country people in particular retained their liking for the strongly flavoured cakes raised with yeast in the traditional manner.

Spiced Dough Cake

10 oz WHITE BREAD FLOUR
2 oz FINE SEMOLINA
3 oz LARD
1 oz FRESH YEAST OR ½ oz DRIED YEAST
8 oz MIXED DRIED FRUIT
3 oz LIGHT SOFT BROWN SUGAR
1 TEASPOON GROUND MIXED SPICE
¼ PINT MILK
2 EGGS

1 · Grease and line an 8 in. round cake tin.
2 · Stir together the flour and semolina and rub in the lard and yeast.
3 · Stir in the fruit, sugar and spice until evenly coloured.
4 · Warm the milk to lukewarm and add to the dry ingredients.
5 · Beat the eggs together and work into the mixture until well blended.
6 · Cover with a clean cloth and leave in a warm place for 45 minutes.
7 · Preheat the oven to moderately hot (400°F/200°C/Gas Mark 6).
8 · Put the mixture into the prepared tin, cover and leave to stand for 15 minutes.
9 · Bake for 45 minutes – 1 hour.
10 · Cool in the tin for 5 minutes, then turn on to a wire rack to cool.
11 · Eat the cake freshly baked, with butter if liked.

This kind of cake was very popular, but it was often known as "baker's cake" and made in a way which was familiar to so many country people who had no oven and relied on the village baker to finish not only cakes but roasts and pies too.

> "It was a great day for tea parties; mothers and sisters and aunts and cousins coming in droves from about the neighbourhood. The chief delicacy at these teas was 'baker's cake', a rich, fruity, spicy dough cake, obtained in the following manner. The house-wife provided all the ingredients excepting the dough, putting raisins and currants, lard, sugar and spice in a basin which she gave to the baker, who added the dough, made and baked the cake, and returned it, beautifully browned in his big oven. The charge was the same as that for a loaf of bread the same size, and the result was delicious. 'There's only one fault wi' these 'ere baker's cakes,' the women used to say; 'they won't keep!' And they would not; they were too good and there were too many children about."
>
> —— *Lark Rise*, Chapter 15

Elaborate and rich cakes were not made in those days, for the cottagers could not afford the ingredients and their ovens were not easy to regulate so that fine baking was out of the question. For special occasions, however, there were tasty plain cakes, based on the original yeast-raised ones, but now using the more modern raising agents. They were frequently made with dripping instead of butter, and were flavoured with a little dried fruit, caraway seeds, spices and cider.

The original fruit used in cakes was the plum in the form of a dried prune. Other dried fruits were gradually added, but any rich fruit cake, bread or pudding retained the name of "plum", and this yeast cake is typical.

Plum Loaf

12 oz SELF-RAISING FLOUR
¼ TEASPOON SALT
¼ TEASPOON GROUND NUTMEG
4 oz BUTTER OR DRIPPING
6 oz CURRANTS
3 oz SULTANAS
3 oz STONED RAISINS
2 oz GLACÉ CHERRIES
2 oz CHOPPED MIXED CANDIED PEEL
6 oz SUGAR
½ PINT MILK
1 oz FRESH YEAST OR ½ oz DRIED YEAST

1 · Grease and line a 2 lb loaf tin.

2 · Sieve the flour, salt and nutmeg into a large bowl. Rub in the butter or dripping until the mixture is like coarse breadcrumbs.

3 · Stir in the currants, sultanas and stoned raisins.

4 · Chop the cherries and stir into the mixture with the peel and sugar.

5 · Heat the milk to lukewarm and stir in the crumbled fresh yeast (or sprinkle on the dried yeast). Leave until frothing and bubbly, which may take up to 15 minutes. Pour on to the dry ingredients and beat well.

6 · Pour into the tin and cover with a piece of greaseproof paper.

7 · Bake in a low oven (300°F/150°C/Gas Mark 2) for 2¼ hours, removing the covering paper after the first hour.

8 · Turn on to a wire rack to cool.

9 · Keep for 2 days before slicing and buttering, or eating plain.

Cut and Come Again Cake

1 lb PLAIN FLOUR
2 TEASPOONS BAKING POWDER
2 TEASPOONS GROUND MIXED SPICE
1 TEASPOON SALT
6 oz BUTTER
6 oz CASTER SUGAR
4 oz RAISINS
4 oz SULTANAS
4 oz CURRANTS
2 EGGS
½ PINT MILK

1 · Line an 8 in. round cake tin with greased greaseproof paper.

2 · Sift the flour, baking powder, spice and salt together.

3 · Rub in the butter until the mixture is like fine breadcrumbs. Stir in the sugar and dried fruit.

4 · Whisk together the eggs and milk and beat into the dry ingredients to make a soft consistency and pour into the tin.

5 · Bake in a moderate oven (350°F/180°C/Gas Mark 4) for 1½ hours.

6 · Leave in the tin for 5 minutes, then turn on to a wire rack to cool.

Vinegar Cake

12 oz PLAIN FLOUR
4 oz BUTTER OR DRIPPING
4 oz SUGAR
3 oz SULTANAS
3 oz CURRANTS
1 oz CHOPPED MIXED CANDIED PEEL
12 TABLESPOONS MILK
½ TEASPOON BICARBONATE OF SODA
1½ TABLESPOONS VINEGAR

1 · Grease and base-line an 8 in. round cake tin.

2 · Sieve the flour and rub in the fat until the mixture is like fine breadcrumbs.

3 · Stir in the sugar, dried fruit and peel.

4 · Mix the soda with a little milk and then add to the rest of the milk and the vinegar.

5 · Mix well and put into the tin.

6 · Bake in a moderate oven (350°F/180°C/Gas Mark 4) for 1½ hours.

7 · Leave in the tin for 5 minutes, then turn on to a wire rack to cool.

This was a popular cake in the winter when eggs were traditionally scarce and expensive, as the vinegar and soda reacted with the milk to help the mixture to rise.

Dripping Cake

8 oz MIXED DRIED FRUIT AND PEEL
5 oz LIGHT SOFT BROWN SUGAR
3 oz BEEF DRIPPING
8 fl oz WATER
8 oz WHOLEMEAL FLOUR
1 TEASPOON BAKING POWDER
½ TEASPOON BICARBONATE OF SODA
PINCH OF GROUND MIXED SPICE
PINCH OF GROUND NUTMEG
PINCH OF GROUND CINNAMON

1 · Grease and base-line a 6 in. round cake tin with greased greaseproof paper.

2 · Put the fruit, sugar and dripping into a thick pan with the water. Bring to the boil and then simmer for 10 minutes. Leave until cool.

3 · Sift together the flour, baking powder, soda and spices. Stir into the fruit mixture, but do not beat.

4 · Put into the tin and bake in a moderate oven (350°F/180°C/Gas Mark 4) for 1-1¼ hours.

5 · Leave in the tin for 5 minutes, then turn on to a wire rack to cool.

When the family pig was killed (Chapter Three), one of the most important jobs was preparing the family's supply of lard, which was used for cooking and for spreading, as well as for making ointments. All the surplus chunks of fat were cut into small pieces and placed in baking tins, which were then heated gently on top of the stove or in a low oven. As the liquid fat drained out, it was poured into jars with sprigs of rosemary for scent and flavour. The fat was heated until every drop of liquid fat had been drained off, and then the pans were full of little crisp pieces of golden-brown fat, known as scratchins, scruggins or crit. These were sprinkled with salt to eat as a treat, or spread on toast. Some were left to get cold and then chopped finely and used in a fruit cake, or mixed with dried fruit in a tart.

Scratchins Cake

1 lb SELF-RAISING FLOUR
8 oz SCRATCHINS (*see above*)
8 oz STONED RAISINS
6 oz DEMERARA SUGAR
GRATED RIND OF 2 LEMONS
1 EGG
¾ PINT SOUR MILK

1 · Grease and base-line a 9 in. round cake tin with greased greaseproof paper.
2 · Sieve the flour.
3 · Cut the scratchins into small pieces and stir into the flour.
4 · Add the raisins, sugar and lemon rind.

5 · Beat the egg and milk together and beat into the dry ingredients. Put into the tin.
6 · Bake in a moderate oven (350°F/ 180°C/Gas Mark 4) for 1½ hours.
7 · Leave in the tin for 10 minutes, then turn on to a wire rack to cool.

"Those old harvest-home feasts created a pleasant warmth for a day. Such a bustling in the farm kitchen for days beforehand – such boiling of hams and roasting of sirloins – such stacks of plum-puddings, made according to the Christmas recipe, piled up in the dairy for heating up on the day – such casks of ale and long plum loaves would astonish any child of this generation."

—— *A Country Calendar*, September

"The honey-bees hurry from flower to flower, as though they knew that the season sped and the time for completing their winter store was limited. I counted five of them, all mealy-winged and thighed, upon the disc of one huge sunflower by the gate today."

—— *A Country Calendar*, August

The gardens were full of bees in the old days, gathering pollen from old-fashioned and highly scented flowers, fruit trees and heather. There were many bee-keepers in the villages, and the bees were treated as friends of the family, who had to be told of a death in the family. The hives were a rich source of honey, which was used as a sweetening agent long before sugar was introduced from the West Indies in the seventeenth century, and some of the best cakes were made with honey.

Plain Honey Cake

8 oz PLAIN FLOUR
1 TEASPOON BAKING POWDER
3 oz BUTTER
3 oz SUGAR
4 oz HONEY
2 EGGS

1 · Grease and base-line a 6 in. round cake tin with greased greaseproof paper.
2 · Sieve the flour and baking powder together.
3 · Cream the butter and sugar together until light and fluffy.
4 · Work in the honey and beaten eggs with a little of the flour. Fold in the remaining flour.
5 · Put into the cake tin and bake in a moderate oven (350°F/180°C/Gas Mark 4) for 1 hour.
6 · Leave in the tin for 5 minutes, then turn on to a wire rack to cool.

Honey Buns

8 oz SELF-RAISING FLOUR
4 oz BUTTER
5 oz HONEY
1 EGG
4 oz SULTANAS

1 · Put the flour into a bowl and rub in the butter until the mixture is like fine breadcrumbs.
2 · Warm the honey to lukewarm.
3 · Beat the egg into the honey and then beat into the flour mixture. The mixture should be stiff, but a little milk may be added if necessary.
4 · Put into greased patty tins and bake in a moderately hot oven (400°F/200°C/Gas Mark 6) for 15 minutes.
5 · Cool on a wire rack.

"Seeing a remembered name over a shop which also displayed a notice of 'Teas' to be had within, Laura entered. The woman who attended to her needs was one of the old Heatherley shopkeepers. She did not recognise Laura, which was not to be wondered at, as to her she must have been but one of many who had come there and gone without leaving behind any special cause for remembrance. When reminded by Laura that she had been a customer of hers of old, she said she had some faint recollection of sending her lunch to the post office. Did she not once complain of too much soda in the rock cakes? The former critic of rock cakes did her best to wipe out the memory of past indiscretions by praising the cake she was then eating."
—— *A Country Calendar*, Post War Pilgrimage

"People used to say then, 'I'd think no more of doing it than of cracking an egg,' little dreaming, dear innocents, that eggs one day would be sixpence each. A penny each for eggs round about Christmas was then thought an exorbitant price. For her big sponge cake, a speciality of hers, Aunt Ann would crack half a dozen. The mixture had to be beaten for half an hour and the children were allowed to take turns at her new patent egg-beater with its handle and revolving wheels."
—— *Over to Candleford*, Chapter 10

Aunt Ann's Sponge

6 EGGS
12 oz CASTER SUGAR
6 oz PLAIN FLOUR
1 oz CORNFLOUR
GRATED RIND OF ½ LEMON
4 ROSE GERANIUM LEAVES (OPTIONAL)

1 · Grease a 9 in. round cake tin with butter and sprinkle evenly with a little flour and cornflour.

2 · Put the egg yolks into a bowl with 6 oz sugar and whisk until white and creamy (the process will be speeded if the bowl is placed over a pan of hot water).

3 · In another bowl, whisk the egg whites to stiff peaks and carefully fold in the remaining sugar.

4 · Sieve the flour and cornflour together.

5 · Fold the egg white mixture and the flour alternately into the egg yolks, and fold in the lemon rind.

6 · Put the rose geranium leaves in the base of the prepared tin and spoon in the cake mixture.

7 · Bake in a moderate oven (325°F/ 160°C/Gas Mark 3) for 1 hour 10 minutes until firm and golden.

8 · Turn on to a wire rack to cool and remove the leaves.

9 · Serve the sponge completely plain except for a little caster sugar sprinkled on the surface. The scented geranium leaves give the cake a most subtle flavour.

"At home she was petted and made much of. She was asked what she would like to eat, instead of being given whatever was on the table, and if the food she fancied were not forthcoming her mother was quite apologetic. But there were delicious things to eat at Cold Harbour. Once, when Laura called for Emily Rose during school holidays they had sponge fingers and cowslip wine, which Emily Rose poured out herself into real wine-glasses."

— *Over to Candleford*, Chapter 13

In Victorian times, coffee was not taken in the middle of the morning, and tea and chocolate were still very expensive. All three drinks were considered to be dangerously stimulating, and the traditional mid-morning refreshment was soothing wine and a plain cake or biscuit. Madeira was often taken, but in the country the more delicate flower wines were enjoyed, with a piece of Madeira or seed cake, a macaroon or a sugared sponge finger.

Sponge Fingers

3 EGGS
2½ oz CASTER SUGAR
2½ oz PLAIN FLOUR
VANILLA ESSENCE

1 · Grease a baking sheet with butter and dust lightly with flour and caster sugar.
2 · Whisk the egg yolks and sugar together until light and fluffy.
3 · Whisk the egg whites to stiff peaks.
4 · Sieve the flour and fold it into the yolks with half the egg whites.

5 · Flavour lightly with vanilla essence.
6 · Fold in the remaining egg whites.
7 · Pipe out finger-lengths of mixture on the baking sheet.
8 · Bake in a moderate oven (350°F/180°C/Gas Mark 4) for 7 minutes.
9 · Cool on a wire rack.

Feasts and fairs were very important to country-dwellers who worked hard for six days each week and never went away for holidays. In *Lark Rise*, Flora Thompson describes many of these occasions, among them Fordlow Feast and its gingerbread stall. Gingerbread had been a treat since medieval times, and was originally a concoction of breadcrumbs, honey and spices, decorated and gilded, which was often given as a present. It was customary to buy gingerbread at fairs to take to those who had not been able to enjoy the fun, often in the form of gingerbread men or babies for the children, and "fairings" or biscuits for adults.

Gingerbread Babies

5 oz DARK SOFT BROWN SUGAR
5 oz BLACK TREACLE
3½ oz BUTTER
1 EGG
1¼ lb PLAIN FLOUR
1 TEASPOON GROUND GINGER
1 TEASPOON GROUND CINNAMON
¼ TEASPOON GROUND CLOVES
½ oz BICARBONATE OF SODA
CURRANTS

If a special cutter is not available, a cardboard shape may be cut out and used, with a big round head, outstretched arms and wide-apart legs.

1 · Heat the sugar and treacle until hot and pour on to the butter. Beat well and cool to lukewarm.
3 · Beat in the egg.
4 · Sieve the flour, spices and soda and mix them to a smooth dough together with the treacle mixture.

4 · Roll out and cut into shapes and put on greased baking sheets.
5 · Put on two currant eyes and three currant buttons.
6 · Bake in a moderate oven (325°F/ 160°C/Gas Mark 3) for 20 minutes.
7 · Lift on to a wire rack to cool.

Fairings

4 oz PLAIN FLOUR
1½ TEASPOONS BICARBONATE OF SODA
¼ TEASPOON GROUND MIXED SPICE
¼ TEASPOON GROUND CINNAMON
¼ TEASPOON GROUND GINGER
PINCH OF SALT
2 oz BUTTER
2 oz DEMERARA SUGAR
2½ TABLESPOONS BLACK TREACLE

1 · Sieve the flour, soda, spices and salt into a bowl.
2 · Rub in the butter until the mixture is like fine breadcrumbs.
3 · Stir in the sugar and treacle and work the dough until it is soft and smooth.
4 · Take rounded teaspoons of the mixture and roll into balls with the hands.
Place on greased baking sheets, leaving room for the biscuits to spread.
5 · Bake in a moderate oven (350°F/ 180°C/Gas Mark 4) for 10 minutes.
6 · Take out of the oven and hit each baking sheet firmly on a solid surface so that the biscuits crack.
7 · Continue baking for 5 minutes.
8 · Leave on the tins for 2-3 minutes, and lift on to a wire rack to cool.

The Larder

"The lavender is but a small part of my harvest. Already my store-cupboard shelves are crowded with jars of jam and jelly and bottled fruit; in corners are roots and seeds, and jars of runner-beans shredded down in brine. Upon the bacon-rack on the kitchen ceiling repose vegetable-marrows enough to feed a garrison. They have been so plentiful here, it was useless trying to give them away. Perhaps, about Christmas time, when vegetables are scarce, some neighbour will deign to accept one. Meanwhile they are a pleasure to look at, glowing mildly yellow through the oaken spars, as comforting as a bowl of daffodils, or a wood fire upon a chilly evening."

—— *A Country Calendar*, September

In the days when there was much visiting between neighbouring houses, and when families were large with cousins and in-laws living nearby, it was wise to keep a good store-cupboard from which sweet and savoury delicacies could be drawn. Prudent housewives saved fruit, vegetables and herbs for winter use, and filled their shelves with jams and pickles. Wild fruit such as blackberries and elderberries, and the more prolific garden fruit like plums, apples and rhubarb were made into large quantities of plain jams and chutneys, but each household had its own specialities. Small amounts of cherries, raspberries, grapes or redcurrants were turned into special preserves to use at teatime when company was expected. Delicate fruit jellies were used to decorate cakes and sweet dishes such as trifles.

Apples were always widely available in the country and Flora Thompson described picking and sorting them with her small boy assistant: "A few of them I shall give away, a few keep for my own use, but the main crop will have to go to the grocer to be transmuted into candles and biscuits and China tea to comfort me in the dark, cold days of winter." *Country Calendar*, September. Her mixed crop of "golden pippins, red and yellow streaked, and the leather-coat russet" was stored in a little loft under one of the gables called "the apple room", or turned into simple preserves.

Potted Apples

4 lb MIXED APPLES
GRANULATED SUGAR
GROUND CLOVES

1 · Cut up the apples without peeling or coring them. Only just cover with water.
2 · Cover and cook in a moderate oven (300°F/150°C/Gas Mark 2) for about 45 minutes until the apples are soft.
3 · Put through a sieve, pressing well to force through all the pulp and juice.
4 · Weigh the purée and add 6 oz sugar and a pinch of cloves to each 1 lb of purée.
5 · Stir over a low heat until the sugar has dissolved Then boil for 5 minutes.
6 · Put into small hot jars and seal tightly.

This makes a good apple sauce for savoury or sweet dishes, or it may be used like a jam and spread on toast or biscuits.

Apple Ginger

3 lb SMALL EATING APPLES
3 lb SUGAR
1½ PINTS WATER
½ oz GROUND GINGER

1 · Peel the apples and remove the cores. Cut the apples into quarters.
2 · Stir the sugar and water together over low heat until the sugar has dissolved. Bring to the boil and simmer gently for 20 minutes.
3 · Add the apples and continue simmering until the apple pieces are transparent and golden.
4 · Stir in the ginger while the apples are cooking. The fruit should remain in neat shapes.
5 · Lift them out with a slotted spoon and put into small screw-top jars.
6 · Bring the syrup to the boil and fill the jars before screwing on lids tightly.
7 · Serve the apple pieces with cream or ice cream as a substitute for stem ginger.

Autumn was always a favourite time with the housewife when wild and garden produce could often be combined, and the rich sweet flavour of blackberries was particularly popular to enhance the blander apples.

"Charity, on her way to afternoon school, had met her in the street, carrying a basket and a hooked stick, and she had said she was going blackberrying. She had been wearing her pink gingham dress and a shady, rush-plaited hat with a wreath of pink rose-buds; the frock, Charity had thought, too good to risk tearing; and when Charity had said, 'How stylish you look!' she had flourished her stick and replied, 'But you see I mean business!' Now Charity felt sure she would find her, picking industriously from the hedge surrounding a copse through which ran a path from the road to the pond, a large, rushy sheet of water, belonging to the Maitlands. It was one of the least frequented spots near the village and the blackberries there grew large and juicy and sweet as sugar and dropped off the briars, for no one went there to pick them; there were plenty nearer home."

—— *Still Glides the Stream*, Chapter 6

Blackberry and Apple Cheese

2 lb MIXED APPLES
¼ PINT WATER
2 lb BLACKBERRIES
GRANULATED SUGAR

1 · Peel and core the apples and cut them into pieces.
2 · Put into a pan with the water and simmer until tender.
3 · Add the berries and simmer until soft.
4 · Sieve the mixture and measure the purée. Allow 1 lb sugar to each pint purée.
5 · Put into a pan and stir over low heat until the sugar has dissolved.
6 · Boil hard until the mixture sets very firmly. Put into warm straight-sided jars and cover.

The "cheese" may be used as a jam, but it used to be turned out of the jars, cut in slices and served with cream. In the eighteenth century, jars were scarce, and the housewife would turn out the preserve, wrap it in oiled paper and store it in a cold place so that the jars were free for another batch.

Rhubarb and Ginger Jam

4 lb RHUBARB
3 lb SUGAR
2 TEASPOONS GROUND GINGER
½ TEASPOON CITRIC ACID

This is a very old-fashioned country favourite and very cheap to make. It may be made at the end of the rhubarb season when the stalks are thick, and rather coarse for other uses.

1 · Wash the rhubarb and cut into 1 in. lengths.
2 · Put into a bowl in layers with the sugar and leave to stand in a cool place, preferably overnight.

3 · Put the mixture into a preserving pan and add the ginger and acid.
4 · Bring to the boil and then boil rapidly to setting point, which will take about 20 minutes after the mixture starts boiling.

The traditional way of judging when setting point has been reached is to pour a spoonful of jam or jelly on to a saucer and then leave it until cold. If setting point has been reached, it will wrinkle when you push it with your finger. But avoid over-boiling which will make jam too syrupy.

Potted Raspberries

4 lb RASPBERRIES
1 oz UNSALTED BUTTER
4 lb CASTER SUGAR

1 · Pick over the fruit, remove any stems or damaged berries.
2 · Rub a preserving pan with the unsalted butter and put in the fruit.
3 · Heat the berries over a low heat until they start to bubble.

4 · While they are heating, put the sugar into a bowl. Leave to warm in a low oven.
5 · Add the sugar to the fruit. Beat with a wooden spoon over very low heat for 15 minutes and put into small hot pots.
6 · Cover and store in a cool place.

It is best to store this preserve for no longer than 6 months, but it is doubtful if anyone will be willing to keep it that long as the flavour is so delicious – just like fresh raspberries.

"Some notable housewives made jelly. Crab-apple jelly was a speciality at the end house. Crab-apple trees abounded in the hedgerows and the children knew just where to go for red crabs, red-and-yellow streaked crabs, or crabs which hung like ropes of green onions on the branches.

It seemed to Laura a miracle when a basket of these, with nothing but sugar and water added, turned into jelly as clear and bright as a ruby. She did not take into account the long stewing, tedious straining, and careful measuring, boiling up and clarifying that went to the filling of the row of glass jars which cast a glow of red light on the whitewash at the back of the pantry shelf."

——— *Lark Rise*, Chapter 6

Crab-Apple Jelly

4 lb CRAB-APPLES
2 PINTS WATER
6 CLOVES
SUGAR

1 · Wash and dry the fruit but do not peel or core.
2 · Cut the apples into quarters and put into a pan with the water and cloves.
3 · Bring to the boil and simmer until the apples are very soft, adding a little more water if the fruit begins to get dry.
4 · Strain through a jelly bag and measure the juice. Allow 1 lb sugar to each pint of juice.
5 · Heat them together gently until the sugar has dissolved.
6 · Boil hard to setting point which will take about 10 minutes (see Rhubarb and Ginger Jam, p. 64).
7 · Pour into small hot jars and cover.

Plum Jam

6 lb PLUMS
1 PINT WATER
6 lb SUGAR

This is delicious if made with a mixture of ripe eating plums with each variety contributing a special flavour and colour.

1 · Halve the plums and remove the stones.
2 · Put fruit and water into a pan and simmer until the fruit is very soft.
3 · Stir in the sugar until dissolved, and then boil hard to setting point.
4 · Pour into hot jars and cover.

Spiced Autumn Jelly

3½ lb ELDERBERRIES
1 lb APPLES
1 lb DAMSONS
1 lb BLACKBERRIES
1 TEASPOON GROUND ALLSPICE
1 TEASPOON GROUND CLOVES
½ TEASPOON GROUND GINGER
PINCH OF GROUND CINNAMON
2 PINTS WATER
SUGAR

1 · Strip the elderberries from their stalks.
2 · Wash and dry the apples but do not peel or core. Cut them into pieces and mix with the elderberries in a pan.
3 · Halve and stone the damsons.
4 · Add damsons and blackberries to the pan with the water and spices.

5 · Simmer for 1 hour until the fruit is soft. Strain through a jelly bag and measure the juice. Allow 1 lb sugar to each pint of juice.
6 · Heat them together gently until the sugar has dissolved. Boil hard to setting point (see Rhubarb and Ginger Jam, p. 64), pour into small hot jars and cover.

Raspberry and Apple Jelly

4 lb RASPBERRIES
2 lb COOKING APPLES
2 PINTS WATER
SUGAR

1 · Put the raspberries into a preserving pan.
2 · Wash the apples and cut them up without peeling or coring.
3 · Add the water and simmer for 1 hour until the fruit is soft.
4 · Strain through a jelly bag and measure

the juice. Allow 1 lb sugar to each pint.
5 · Heat them together gently until the sugar has dissolved.
6 · Boil hard to setting point (see Rhubarb and Ginger Jam, p. 64), which will take about 10 minutes.
7 · Pour into small hot jars and cover.

It is difficult to set jam or jelly which contains only raspberries, but the apples provide essential acid and pectin and do not detract from the delicious raspberry flavour.

Gooseberry and Elderflower Jelly

4 lb GREEN GOOSEBERRIES
1 BUNCH ELDERFLOWER HEADS
SUGAR

1 · Wash the gooseberries but do not top and tail them. Put into a pan with just enough water to cover.
2 · Simmer for 1 hour until the fruit is very soft.
3 · Strain through a jelly bag and measure the juice. Allow 1 lb sugar to each pint.
4 · Put the juice and sugar into a pan and add the elderflower heads tied in a piece of muslin or thin cloth. Heat gently until the sugar has dissolved.
5 · Boil hard to setting point (see Rhubarb and Ginger Jam, p. 64) which will take about 10 minutes.
6 · Remove the elderflower heads. Pour into small hot jars and cover.

This gives a pale green jelly which tastes of muscat grapes (elderflowers and gooseberries are in season together and are traditional culinary companions).

Mint or Parsley Jelly Omit the elderflower heads, but use a large bunch of mint or parsley instead. Just before setting point is reached, remove the bunch of herbs, and stir in plenty of chopped mint or parsley. Serve with lamb or ham.

Spiced Redcurrant Jelly

3 lb REDCURRANTS
1 PINT WATER
¼ PINT WHITE VINEGAR
3 CLOVES
½ CINNAMON STICK
SUGAR

1 · Strip the redcurrants from their stems and put into a pan with the water and vinegar.
2 · Tie the spices in a piece of muslin or thin cloth and hang them in the pan.
3 · Simmer until the fruit is soft.
4 · Remove the spice bag and strain the fruit through a jelly bag.
5 · Measure the juice and allow 1 lb sugar to each pint of juice.
6 · Heat the juice gently with the sugar until the sugar has dissolved.
7 · Boil hard to setting point (see Rhubarb and Ginger Jam, p. 64), which will take about 10 minutes.
8 · Pour into small hot jars and cover.

This is not as sweet as the usual redcurrant jelly, and it is delicious with lamb or game.

"At home, the plums on the front wall of the house were ripe, and the warm, fruity smell of boiling jam drew all the wasps in the neighbourhood. Other jams, jellies and pickles already stood on the pantry shelves. Big yellow vegetable marrows dangled from hooks, and ropes of onions and bunches of drying thyme and sage."

—— *Over to Candleford*, Chapter 13

The sheer lushness of garden and hedgerow meant that the housewife was kept very busy storing every scrap of valuable food. With no refrigeration or freezing equipment, everything had to go into stone jars or bottles. Big earthenware pots were commonly used for jam and salted vegetables, although more delicate jams and jellies went into small glass jars covered with white paper dipped in brandy which aided preservation. Stone jars, which were also used for fruit bottling, were covered with airtight pig's bladders, but towards the end of the century, tall green glass jars were introduced with glass lids and screw-tops. As well as basic pickles and chutneys, spiced fruits were popular for special occasions either to accompany meat or poultry, or to use as an emergency sweet dish.

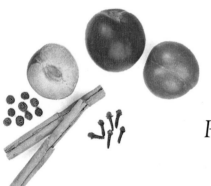

Pickled Plums

2 lb PLUMS
1 PINT VINEGAR
1½ lb SUGAR
1 in. CINNAMON STICK
1 TEASPOON CLOVES
10 ALLSPICE BERRIES
BLADE OF MACE

1 · The best plums to use are small black eating ones. Wipe them and prick each one 4 times with a needle (do this over a bowl so that no juice is lost). Put into a bowl.

2 · Boil the vinegar, sugar and spices together for 10 minutes, pour over the plums and leave overnight.

3 · Drain off the liquid and boil for 10 minutes. Pour over the fruit and leave for 12 hours.

4 · Put the plums and liquid into a pan and bring to the boil. Discard the spices.

5 · Lift out the plums and pack into preserving jars.

6 · Boil the syrup and pour over the plums to cover them. Seal the jars with vinegar-proof lids.

7 · Serve with pork, ham or poultry.

Mustard Pickle

1 MEDIUM MARROW
1 MEDIUM CAULIFLOWER
1 CUCUMBER
1 lb FRENCH BEANS
1 lb SMALL ONIONS
1 oz COOKING SALT
10 oz SUGAR
2 PINTS VINEGAR
2 oz PLAIN FLOUR
2 oz MUSTARD POWDER
½ oz TURMERIC POWDER
½ oz GROUND GINGER
½ oz GROUND NUTMEG

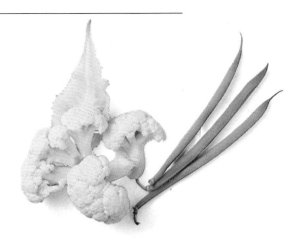

1 · Do not peel the marrow, but remove seeds and fibrous interior. Chop the flesh into small pieces.
2 · Cut the cauliflower into small florets.
4 · Dice the cucumber and cut the beans into chunks.
5 · Peel the onions.
6 · Mix the vegetables in a bowl, sprinkle with salt, cover with cold water and leave to soak overnight. Drain off the liquid.
7 · Mix all the dry ingredients and a little of the vinegar to make a smooth paste.
8 · Put the vegetables into a pan with the remaining vinegar and simmer until tender but unbroken.
9 · Add a little of the hot vinegar to the blended dry ingredients and then stir into the vegetables.
10 · Simmer for 10 minutes, stirring all the time, until thick.
11 · Put into preserving jars and cover with vinegar-proof lids.

Pickled Beetroot

8 MEDIUM BEETROOT
1½ PINTS MALT VINEGAR
½ oz BLACK PEPPERCORNS
½ oz ALLSPICE BERRIES
1 TEASPOON SALT

1 · Scrub the beetroot lightly and put into a large pan.
2 · Cover with cold water and a lid, bring to the boil and simmer for 45 minutes. Leave to cool in the cooking liquid.
3 · Rub off the stems, roots and skin, and slice or dice the beetroot.
4 · Pack into a preserving jar.
5 · Put the vinegar, spices and salt into a pan and bring to the boil.
6 · Leave until cold and pour over the beetroot to cover completely, leaving in the spices.
7 · Seal the jar tightly with a vinegar-proof lid.

Pickled Onions

2 lb SMALL ONIONS
1½ oz COOKING SALT
1½-2 PINTS MALT VINEGAR
¼ oz CINNAMON STICK
¼ oz BLADE MACE
¼ oz ALLSPICE BERRIES
¼ oz BLACK PEPPERCORNS
¼ oz WHOLE CLOVES

1 · Peel the onions and put them on a shallow earthenware dish.
2 · Sprinkle with salt and leave in a cool place overnight.
3 · Rinse in cold water, drain well and pack into a preserving jar, pushing the onions down lightly with the handle of a wooden spoon so that there are no large spaces.
4 · Put the vinegar and spices into a pan and bring to the boil.
5 · Leave until cold and strain over the onions to cover them completely.
6 · Seal tightly with a vinegar-proof lid. Keep for 3-4 weeks before using.

Pickled Eggs

12 EGGS
2 PINTS WINE VINEGAR
½ oz ROOT GINGER
½ oz MUSTARD SEEDS
½ oz WHITE PEPPERCORNS
2 CHILLIES

In the old days, eggs were widely available in spring and summer, and very cheap, so it was prudent to try to preserve them for winter. Pickled eggs were a popular delicacy to eat with crusty bread or a salad.

1 · Hard-boil the eggs, cool and shell them.
2 · Pack them upright in a wide-mouthed jar and place the chillies on top.
3 · Simmer the vinegar with bruised ginger, mustard seeds and peppercorns for 5 minutes. Strain and cool.
4 · When cold, pour over the eggs and seal tightly with a vinegar-proof lid.
5 · Keep for 2-3 weeks before using.

Gooseberry Chutney

4 lb GREEN GOOSEBERRIES
1 lb DARK SOFT BROWN SUGAR
2 PINTS VINEGAR
1 lb ONIONS
1½ lb SEEDLESS RAISINS
4 oz SALT
2 oz GROUND ALLSPICE
1 oz MUSTARD POWDER

1 · Top and tail the gooseberries.
2 · Mix the sugar with half the vinegar and simmer until the sugar has dissolved.
3 · Boil the gooseberries in the remaining vinegar until soft and broken.
4 · Chop the onions finely and add them to the vinegar syrup together with the raisins, spices and salt.
5 · Simmer for 5 minutes.
6 · Put the two mixtures together and simmer for 1 hour until golden and thick, stirring occasionally to prevent sticking.
7 · Put into jars and seal with vinegar-proof lids.

Grape and Apple Chutney

2 lb WHITE GRAPES
2 lb COOKING APPLES
6 oz SEEDLESS RAISINS
1½ lb LIGHT SOFT BROWN SUGAR
½ PINT CIDER VINEGAR
¼ PINT LEMON JUICE
GRATED RIND OF 1 LEMON
¼ TEASPOON GROUND GINGER
¼ TEASPOON SALT
¼ TEASPOON PAPRIKA
¼ TEASPOON GROUND CINNAMON
½ TEASPOON ALLSPICE BERRIES
½ TEASPOON CLOVES

If possible, use small seedless grapes. If they are not in season, the grapes must be cut in half and the pips removed.

1 · Do not peel the apples, but remove the cores, and chop the flesh finely.
2 · Put the grapes, apples, raisins, sugar, vinegar, lemon juice and rind, ginger, salt, paprika and cinnamon into a thick-based saucepan.
3 · Tie the remaining spices in a piece of muslin and hang them in the mixture.
4 · Bring to the boil, stirring well, and then reduce heat and simmer for about 1 hour until thick.
5 · Remove the spice bag.
6 · Put chutney into hot screw-top jars and seal with vinegar-proof lids.

Rhubarb Chutney

2 lb RHUBARB
8 oz ONIONS
1½ lb DARK SOFT BROWN SUGAR
8 oz SULTANAS
1 PINT VINEGAR
½ oz MUSTARD POWDER
1 TEASPOON GROUND MIXED SPICE
1 TEASPOON GROUND BLACK PEPPER
1 TEASPOON GROUND GINGER
1 TEASPOON SALT
PINCH OF CAYENNE PEPPER

This is a very good way of using up old rhubarb at the end of the summer when it has become too coarse for table use.

1 · Wipe the rhubarb and cut into small pieces.
2 · Chop the onions finely.
3 · Put the rhubarb, onions and the remaining ingredients into a pan. Stir well and simmer until golden and thick, which will take about 1 hour. Stir occasionally to prevent sticking.
4 · Put into jars and seal with vinegar-proof lids.

Spiced Prunes

1 lb LARGE TENDER PRUNES
¾ PINT MILKLESS TEA
1 PINT WHITE VINEGAR
1 lb SUGAR
10 ALLSPICE BERRIES
1 TEASPOON CLOVES
1 in. CINNAMON STICK
BLADE OF MACE

1 · Put the prunes into a bowl and cover with the tea. Soak overnight and then simmer in the tea until the prunes are plump.
2 · In another pan, boil the vinegar, sugar and spices together for 5 minutes.
3 · Add the prunes and cooking liquid and continue simmering for 7 minutes.
4 · Lift out the prunes with a slotted spoon and put into small preserving jars.
5 · Bring the cooking liquid to the boil, pour over the prunes to cover them and seal the jars tightly.

These prunes keep for years, and are very good with fat meats such as pork, ham or goose.

"In one little roadside dell mushrooms might sometimes be found, small button mushrooms with beaded moisture on their cold milk-white skins. The dell was the farthest point of their walk; after searching the long grass for mushrooms, in season and out of season – for they would not give up hope – they turned back and never reached the second milestone.

Once or twice when they reached the dell they got a greater thrill than even the discovery of a mushroom could give; for the gipsies were there . . ."

——— *Lark Rise*, Chapter 2

Potted Mushrooms

1 lb MUSHROOMS
2 oz BUTTER
SALT AND PEPPER
PINCH OF GROUND NUTMEG
2 oz CLARIFIED BUTTER (p. 23)

The best mushrooms to use for this dish are the large open caps – field or horse mushrooms are particularly good.

1 · Trim the ends of the stems and then pull off the stems and cut each one into two.

2 · Wipe the mushrooms clean but do not wash them as they absorb water which spoils their texture and flavour and destroys the keeping quality of the preserve.

3 · Cut the mushrooms in quarters.

4 · Melt the butter in a thick saucepan and add the mushroom caps and stems. Shake the pan gently over low heat for 3 minutes.

5 · Season well and continue simmering and shaking the pan until the mushrooms are very soft.

6 · Drain the mushrooms (the liquid is excellent for soup or gravy). Leave until cold and press into small pots.

7 · Pour on melted clarified butter.

8 · Serve cold with toast, or store in the refrigerator (up to 3 days) or in the freezer (up to 2 months) for adding to recipes together with the butter in which they are preserved.

Late in the autumn, Christmas preparations started, using the apples which were in store. Rich fruited mincemeat was essential for the feasting.

Christmas Mincemeat

1 lb CURRANTS
1 lb SULTANAS
1 lb SEEDED RAISINS
1½ lb BEEF SUET
1 lb DARK SOFT BROWN SUGAR
1 oz GROUND MIXED SPICE
1 lb PREPARED APPLES
GRATED RIND OF 2 ORANGES
GRATED RIND OF 2 LEMONS
¼ PINT BRANDY
¼ PINT RUM

This mincemeat is most delicious when made with big sticky raisins which have to be seeded, and a lump of suet from the butcher which must be grated by hand, but it takes very little time to make and is far superior to any bought variety.

1 · Put the currants and sultanas into a large bowl.
2 · Remove the pips from the raisins and chop the fruit.
3 · Add to the bowl with the grated suet, sugar and spice.
4 · Weigh the apples carefully after peeling and coring.

5 · Mince them, saving all the juice which runs out.
6 · Mix in with the other ingredients and add the fruit rinds and spirits.
7 · Mix very thoroughly and put into clean sterilised jars with screw-tops.
8 · Store in a cool place. Stir well before using.

Women never worked in the vegetable gardens or allotments, for there was a strict division of labour and that was "men's work". Most of the houses had at least a narrow flower border beside the pathway, but there was little money to spare for plants or seeds, and women depended on roots and cuttings given by their neighbours, so that there was little variety between the gardens.

"As well as their flower garden, the women cultivated a herb corner, stocked with thyme and parsley, and sage for cooking, rosemary to flavour the home-made lard, lavender to scent the best clothes, and peppermint, pennyroyal, horehound, camomile, tansy, balm, and rue for physic."

—— *Lark Rise*, Chapter 6

These herbs were essential to make simple food interesting, but they were also loved for their scent. In *Still Glides the Stream* old Uncle Reuben always went to church carrying "in his hand or his buttonhole a stalk or two of lavender, or a sprig of southernwood, thyme or some other sweet-smelling herb. In his childhood it had been a general custom to carry such sprigs of sweet herbs to church, and he loved to keep up the old country ways, including regular churchgoing."

Sprigs of lavender or rosemary were tucked into boxes of sugar and, after a few weeks, the scented sugar could be used for cakes or delicate sweet dishes. Leaves of the fragrant cottage geraniums were used to flavour crab-apple jelly, or placed under the cake mixture in a tin to give a deliciously elusive flavour to sugared sponges. Favourite garden herbs were tied into paper bags and dried to store in the larder, sometimes in cunning blends which could be used quickly to give subtlety to savoury dishes and stuffings.

Many of these seasonings have been hallowed by time, according to what has been easily available in the store cupboard or garden. Old-fashioned housewives kept spice cupboards or boxes near the stove so that they could add their favourite "pinches" easily while cooking. They could pick a few sage leaves in the garden to pair with onions in a stuffing for rich meats such as pork or duck, recognising that the essential oils in the herb helped the family to digest fatty meats. Since citrus fruit was highly seasonal and expensive, they dried the peel or steeped it in spirit or sugar so that the flavourings of orange or lemon could be used right through the year in cakes or puddings.

These subtle flavourings are easily prepared at home, and give a far more interesting seasoning to everyday dishes than the commercial equivalents.

Sweet Herb Mixture

2 oz DRIED PARSLEY
2 oz DRIED MARJORAM
2 oz DRIED CHERVIL
1 oz DRIED THYME
1 oz DRIED LEMON THYME
1 oz DRIED BASIL
1 oz DRIED SUMMER SAVORY
½ oz DRIED TARRAGON

1 · The herbs are best dried by tying in small bunches and hanging in a cool, dry, airy place until crisp. The leaves should then be removed from the stems.

2 · Mix the leaves together and rub them into a coarse powder between the hands.

3 · Store in an airtight jar.

4 · To use the seasoning, add a couple of pinches to a recipe when mixed herbs are required.

Kitchen Pepper

6 oz SALT
1 oz GROUND GINGER
½ oz GROUND BLACK PEPPER
½ oz GROUND NUTMEG
½ oz GROUND MACE
½ oz GROUND CLOVES

1 · Mix thoroughly together and store in an airtight jar or tin.

2 · Add a little to sauces and gravy.

Mustard was a popular spice, perhaps because it went so well with the rich pork dishes and fatty fish which were an important part of the country diet. Mustard powder was available, but a fuller flavour was obtained from brown or white mustard seeds, pounded with a pestle and mortar after soaking overnight. Mustard seeds may now be bought from grocers, chemists and health food shops.

Household Mustard

2 oz WHITE MUSTARD SEEDS
½ PINT WATER
2 TEASPOONS SEA SALT
8 TABLESPOONS WINE VINEGAR
SALT AND PEPPER

1 · Put the mustard seeds into a bowl.
2 · Boil the water and sea salt and leave until lukewarm.
3 · Pour over the seeds and leave overnight.
4 · Drain well and crush the seeds until creamy (this may be done in a blender or small coffee grinder).
5 · Bring the vinegar to the boil, leave until lukewarm, and then work into the mustard drop by drop to make a thick cream.
6 · Season with pepper and a little salt.
7 · Put into a small pot and cover.

Summer Herb Mustard

2 oz MUSTARD SEEDS
4 SPRIGS CHERVIL
1 SPRIG BASIL
1 SMALL SPRIG FENNEL
1 SPRIG MARJORAM
3 JUNIPER BERRIES
1 TABLESPOON REDCURRANT JELLY
2 TEASPOONS OLIVE OIL
8 TABLESPOONS WINE VINEGAR
SALT AND PEPPER

1 · Crush the mustard seeds without soaking them.
2 · Strip the herb leaves from their stems and chop the leaves finely.
3 · Crush the juniper berries.
4 · Work the herbs and juniper berries into the redcurrant jelly and then gradually work in the mustard seeds and olive oil.
5 · Boil the vinegar and leave until lukewarm, then work into the mustard drop by drop.
6 · Season with salt and pepper to taste.
7 · Put into a pot and cover. Leave for 4-5 days before using.

Extra Strong Mustard

2 oz WHITE MUSTARD SEEDS
½ TEASPOON GROUND NUTMEG
1 LARGE PINCH GROUND ALLSPICE
½ TEASPOON GRATED HORSERADISH
8 TABLESPOONS WHITE WINE VINEGAR
SALT AND PEPPER

1 · Crush the mustard seeds without soaking them.
2 · Mix with the other ingredients and heat gently over low heat until creamy.
3 · Leave until cold and put into a pot.
4 · Cover and leave for 8 days before using.

This mustard is particularly good to serve with ham or beef.

Winter Mint Sauce

¼ PINT FRESH MINT LEAVES
½ PINT VINEGAR
6 oz DEMERARA SUGAR

1 · Chop the mint very finely and press into a measuring jug to find the correct quantity.

2 · Put the vinegar and sugar into a pan and heat slowly so that the sugar dissolves.

3 · Boil for 2 minutes and stir in the mint.

4 · Leave until cold.

5 · Put into small screw-top jars and seal with vinegar-proof lids.

6 · To use the sauce, spoon out the required amount of the mixture and add a little more vinegar.

Huge quantities of vinegar were used for preservation, and many country housewives who brewed their own beer used a method of acidifying the liquid to make vinegar. Wine was also used, and it is more convenient today to make vinegar with a curious natural agent called a "vinegar mother". This method ensures a permanent vinegar supply and needs no elaborate equipment.

A large container is the only requirement. This may either be a wooden barrel on legs, holding 7 or 8 pints, or a stone jar with a lid and a bung tap a few inches above the base (both of these may be obtained from a shop which specialises in wine-making supplies).

When choosing a stone jar, make sure that the tap is not right at the bottom, as there must always be a depth of vinegar on which the "mother" can swim. The hole at the top of the jar should be wide, with a loosely fitting lid or cork, as air must be able to enter the container, but the jar must be covered so that the tiny flies commonly known as vinegar-flies do not enter. Before using the container, rinse the inside completely with a little wine or boiled vinegar. Find an undisturbed place to keep the vinegar jar – a warm but shady windowsill is ideal – but do not store the jar in a wine cellar or cupboard, as the presence of the vinegar can contaminate the wine and turn that into vinegar too. The only other equipment needed is a selection of bottles into which the vinegar can be drawn off and then flavoured.

When preparing the vinegar, the same-coloured wine and vinegar, i.e. white or red, must be used, and the amount of wine drawn off must be replaced with an equal quantity of the same-coloured wine. It is important not to drown the vinegar mother, which floats on the surface of the vinegar. This means pouring the replacement wine very gently down the inside of the jar so that the "mother" is not disturbed. As well as replacing the vinegar with a quantity of wine, the remains of bottles may be added after meals if they are unlikely to be used quickly for cooking purposes.

The Vinegar Mother

To prepare a "mother of vinegars" which will go on living for many years, use a cheap, rather acid wine, and a good wine vinegar to start the process, matching red wine with red wine vinegar, and white wine with white wine vinegar. Prepare the container, rinsing very thoroughly with a little wine or boiled vinegar, and discard the rinsing liquid. Take 1¾ pints wine and one-quarter that amount of wine vinegar. Mix together and pour into the container. Put on the lid, or cork lightly, and open every two days for air to penetrate. When opening, cover the top with a piece of muslin or thin cloth so that insects do not enter the jar. After about two weeks, there will be a dark, thick, viscous skin on top of the liquid, and this is the "mother". When wine is put into contact with the "mother", it becomes vinegar. Test the resulting vinegar once the "mother" has formed, after about three weeks, by draining off a little from the tap. If it has reached the preferred acidity, drain off nearly all the vinegar, and then carefully top up the jar with the same quantity of wine.

From then on, the vinegar may be taken off as and when wanted, so long as it is always replaced with the equivalent amount of wine. The drawn-off vinegar should be kept in corked or screw-topped bottles, and flavoured as required. Flavouring should not be put into the main vinegar container or it will be tainted.

Flavoured Vinegars

Home-made vinegar or commercial wine vinegar may be flavoured with herbs, fruit or flowers, and these special vinegars give subtle distinction to salad dressings, mayonnaise or sauces made from them. Often flavoured and sweetened vinegars were used to make refreshing summer drinks, or soothing winter potions. Strongly flavoured fruits such as raspberries, gooseberries, blackcurrants and blackberries were commonly used for this purpose, or delicate flowers such as primroses, cowslips, roses, violets, carnations and elderflowers.

For a simple flavoured vinegar, try spearing lemon slices or shallots on a wooden skewer and leave in a bottle of wine vinegar. Alternatives are a few garlic cloves in a bottle, or a large sprig of fennel, rosemary, tarragon, thyme or mint. For a lightly flavoured vinegar, put a handful of herbs into each bottle, and drain off the vinegar after a week, rebottling without herbs.

Flower Vinegar

1 oz FLOWER HEADS
1 PINT WHITE WINE VINEGAR

Delicately flavoured flower vinegars are excellent for salads, and like the herb variety are best prepared with white wine vinegar. The best flowers to use are old-fashioned scented roses, elderflowers, thyme flowers, violets, carnations and basil flowers.

1 · Spread the flowers on a piece of clean paper and dry in a sunny place for 2 days (a sunny windowsill is the ideal place).
2 · Put the dried flowers into a preserving jar or large bottle with the vinegar and seal tightly.
3 · Leave in the sun for 15 days before straining, bottling and labelling.

Summer Garden Vinegar

5 PINTS RED OR WHITE WINE VINEGAR
1 HANDFUL TARRAGON
1 HANDFUL SCENTED ROSE PETALS
1 HANDFUL NASTURTIUM LEAVES
1 HANDFUL FENNEL
2 GARLIC CLOVES
10 SHALLOTS OR SMALL ONIONS
1 LARGE SPRIG THYME
3 BAY LEAVES
3 CLOVES
1 oz SALT
1 oz ELDERFLOWERS

The quantities for this recipe are large as the essential ingredients are only available during a short summer season, but this delicious vinegar is worth making for winter use.

1 · Put the vinegar into a large bowl with the tarragon, rose petals, nasturtiums and fennel.
2 · Add peeled garlic and shallots or on-ions and the remaining ingredients.
3 · Cover with a cloth and leave to stand for 4 weeks.
4 · Strain into bottles and label.

Spiced Vinegar

2 PINTS VINEGAR
2 oz CLOVES
¼ oz BLADE MACE
¼ oz CINNAMON STICK

1 · Heat the vinegar just to boiling point.
2 · Pour into a bowl and add the spices.

3 · Cover and leave in a warm place.
4 · After a week strain and bottle.

Herb Vinegar

SMALL BUNCH OF HERBS
1 BOTTLE WHITE WINE VINEGAR

A herb vinegar is best made with white wine vinegar, as the pale colour is most suitable for dressings and the flavour is delicate. Use herbs which have a distinctive flavour such as basil, mint, thyme, fennel, marjoram, sage, rosemary, tarragon or garlic.

1 · Take 3 tablespoons vinegar from the bottle and replace with a small bunch of the chosen herb (or 2 large peeled and bruised garlic cloves).

2 · Screw on the lid tightly and keep for 1 month, shaking the bottle occasionally.
3 · Remove the bunch of herbs and put in a small fresh sprig for identification.

Strong Garlic Vinegar

1 PINT RED OR WHITE WINE VINEGAR
2 LARGE GARLIC CLOVES
1 SMALL ONION
1 BAY LEAF
1 SPRIG TARRAGON
2 CLOVES
PINCH OF GROUND NUTMEG
PINCH OF SALT

This is a richly flavoured vinegar which is useful for robust sauces and dressings.

1 · Put the vinegar into a screw-top jar.
2 · Add the crushed garlic and finely chopped onion with the other ingredients.

3 · Seal tightly and leave in the sun for 21 days.
4 · Strain into a bottle and label.

A head of elderflowers and a sprig of mint can be substituted instead of the bay leaf.

Wines, Beers and Cordials

"**E**lderberry wine was brought out in the tall glass decanter only used on special occasions, and biscuits and filberts and apples were placed on the table in the old-fashioned green leaf-shaped dessert dishes which had belonged to the girls' grandmother. To Reuben the occasion seemed to demand something even more special. He went to the cupboard known as 'Dad's' and brought out a dusty black bottle. 'Here's something you've not tasted on all your travels, a drop of fine old metheglin,' he told Oliver. ''Tis the last bottle of the half-dozen your Aunt Marianna made the first year of our marriage. I'd meant it for Bess's wedding, but somehow forgot all about it; maybe because it didn't seem to mix well with Arnold's champagne. I'm not going to offer you girls any; 'tis too strong and heady for maidens and you'd best stick to your wine.' He poured three glasses for the men of the party, then, holding his own glass to the light and closing one eye, the better to focus the dark amber liquid, he said, 'Here's welcome home to the warrior, love to the absent, fond memories of our lost ones, and good luck to us all!' and they honoured the old country toast by draining their glasses."

—— *Still Glides the Stream*, Chapter 11

Home-made alcoholic drinks, soft drinks and cordials were enjoyed by men, women and children in the days when tea, coffee and chocolate were extremely expensive and only indulged in for very special occasions. When a poor family had any tea, the leaves would be used over and over again, and even when drained of all goodness would finally be used for cleaning floors and carpets.

Beer was the universal drink, taken at breakfast by people of all ages, and forming part of the victuals of children away at school. In large houses and farmhouses, beer and cider would be prepared in a brewhouse, but there were many refreshing substitutes which could be more easily and quickly prepared. Nettle beer and a light hop beer for instance took little time to make and were appreciated for their quality of purifying the blood and clearing the system in springtime. At harvest, these drinks were refreshing without being intoxicating.

Light fizzy drinks such as sherbet and ginger beer gave pleasure to children, while apples, rhubarb, elderflowers and citrus fruit added their delicious flavours to soft drinks which helped to digest the often heavy foods which were normally served to most families.

The elder tree had a bad reputation as a witches' tree, because the wood had been used for the Cross, but the low scrubby bushes grew everywhere and provided scented water for the complexion and ointment for soothing. Both flowers and berries were used for delicious wine.

"The same old lady used to make a wine from the flowers. This was called 'ladies' elder wine', the 'gentlemen's' being the strong, heady beverage, much like port, which was brewed from the berries in autumn. The wine made from the flowers was a sparkling drink, very light and harmless, which was brought out and handed with a sponge finger to lady and children callers, that they might sip genteelly and not find the time long while their hostess hunted up the requisite number of eggs from the nest, or weighed the honey or clotted-cream they had come to purchase."

———— *A Country Calendar*, July

Gentlemen's Elder Wine

4 lb ELDERBERRIES
8 PINTS WATER
1 LEMON
½ oz ROOT GINGER
1 SMALL STICK CINNAMON
¼ oz CLOVES
3 lb DEMERARA SUGAR
8 oz STONED RAISINS
1 TEASPOON YEAST

1 · Weigh the fruit without stalks.
2 · Mash in a large bowl and pour on boiling water.
3 · Cover with a clean cloth and leave to stand for 2 days, stirring daily.
4 · Strain through muslin into a clean bowl.
5 · Slice the lemon without peeling.
6 · Bruise the ginger with a hammer.
7 · Tie the lemon pieces and ginger into a muslin bag with the cinnamon and cloves.
8 · Put the spices into a pan with 1 pint of the elderberry liquid. Bring to the boil and boil for 20 minutes.

9 · Leave until cold and add the liquid to the rest of the elderberry juice.
10 · Stir the sugar, chopped raisins and yeast into the liquid. Cover with a clean cloth and leave in a warm room until the liquid has ceased forming bubbles and fermenting, which will take about 6 days.
11 · Strain into a clean jar and fit with a sterilised cork.
12 · Store for 6 months.
13 · Put into a clean jar, cork and store for 6 more months.
14 · Put into bottles and keep for 3 years before using.

This wine is rich in tannin and will have the best flavour if made with well-ripened berries. It matures to a smooth richness like port, and is particularly enjoyed served warm on a cold winter evening.

Ladies' Elder Wine

4 ELDERFLOWER HEADS
1½ lb SUGAR
2 TABLESPOONS WHITE VINEGAR
8 PINTS COLD WATER
2 LEMONS

1 · Put the elderflowers, sugar, vinegar and water into a large bowl.
2 · Cut the lemons in half and squeeze the juice into a bowl.
3 · Cut the lemon halves into large pieces and add to the bowl. Cover with a clean cloth and leave to stand for 24 hours, stirring occasionally.
4 · Strain and pour into screw-top cider or beer bottles.

This is ready to drink in 5 or 6 days, and is light and effervescent with the delicate flavour of muscat grapes.

Mead is usually defined as a fermentation of honey and water, which tastes like wine, and has no additional herbs, spices, fruit juices or vegetable extracts. Metheglin is, strictly speaking, a honey-based liquor which has been fermented and in which spices are used. Both drinks are very old and were drunk at festivals and weddings. Celebrations of the latter often lasted a full month, and this was said to give rise to the word "honeymoon".

"Some of the older people who kept bees made mead, known there as 'metheglin'. It was a drink almost superstitiously esteemed, and the offer of a glass was regarded as a great compliment. Those who made it liked to make a little mystery of the process; but it was really very simple. Three pounds of honey were allowed to every gallon of spring water. This had to be running spring water, and was obtained from a place in the brook where the water bubbled up; never from the well. The honey and water were boiled together, and skimmed and strained and worked with a little yeast; then kept in a barrel for six months, when the metheglin was ready for bottling.

Old Sally said that some folk messed up their metheglin with lemons, bay leaves and suchlike; but all she could say was that folks who'd add anything to honey didn't deserve to have bees to work for them.

Old metheglin was supposed to be the most intoxicating drink on earth, and it was certainly potent, as a small girl once found when, staying up to welcome home a soldier uncle from Egypt, she was invited to take a sip from his glass and took a pull."

—— *Lark Rise*, Chapter 6

Mead

3 lb CRYSTALLINE HONEY
½ oz YEAST
WATER

Traditionally, mead is made with soft water, and clean filtered rain water is ideal.

1 · Put the honey into a large bowl and gradually add water, mixing well until the honey is dissolved.
2 · Add enough water to make the total volume up to 8 pints.
3 · Bring to the boil and simmer for exactly 5 minutes, and then leave to cool.
4 · Strain through a jelly bag or piece of clean cloth into a fermentation jar and add the yeast to the lukewarm liquid.
5 · Cover with a clean cloth and leave for 3 days until the vigorous fermentation dies down.
6 · Insert an airlock and keep in a warm place until fermentation ceases.
7 · Leave in a cool place for 1 month and syphon off into clean bottles and cork them firmly.

This produces a dry mead, and a sweeter version may be made by using 4 lb honey. If liquid honey is used, add an extra 8 oz. The best mead matures for 7 years before using.

Metheglin

5 lb HONEY
8 PINTS WATER
1 LEMON
1 SPRIG ROSEMARY
1 SPRIG LEMON BALM
½ oz ROOT GINGER
¾ oz YEAST

1 · Put the water into a large pan and add the lemon peel which should be very thin.
2 · Add the herbs and crushed ginger and simmer for 20 minutes.
3 · Strain and pour over honey.
4 · Mix well and when lukewarm add the lemon juice and yeast.
5 · Cover the pan and leave to ferment for 24 hours.
6 · Put into a fermentation jar and insert an airlock.
7 · Leave in a warm place until fermentation finishes, then leave in a cool place for 3 weeks.
8 · Syphon into clean bottles and cork them firmly.

The flavour of the metheglin may be varied by using an orange instead of lemon, or by adding cinnamon or cloves, or by using marjoram and rue.

"Miss Lane could remember when all the beer for the house and the smiths was brewed there. In Laura's time it came from the brewery in nine-gallon casks. The custom of home brewing was fading out in farmers' and tradesmen's households; it saved trouble and expense to buy the beer from the brewery in barrels; but a few belonging to the older generation still brewed at home for themselves and their workmen. At the Candleford Green Post Office, Laura issued about half a dozen four-shilling home-brewing licences a year. One woman there kept an off-licence and brewed her own beer. There was a large old yew tree at the bottom of her garden, and her customers sat beneath its spreading branches on the green, just outside her garden wall, and consumed their drinks 'off the premises' in compliance with the law. But, as she brewed for sale, hers must have been a more expensive licence, probably issued by the magistrates."

——— *Candleford Green*, Chapter 3

While few people were still brewing their own beer from malt and hops, most households made lighter beers which matured quickly, were not too intoxicating and were very refreshing, particularly at harvest time when throats became very dry.

Hop Beer

1 lb HOPS
8 PINTS WATER
1 lb LIGHT SOFT BROWN SUGAR
½ oz FRESH YEAST

1 · Put the hops and water into a large pan and boil together for 40 minutes.
2 · Strain and stir in the sugar.
3 · When lukewarm, sprinkle in the yeast.

4 · Cover and leave in a warm place.
5 · After 24 hours skim and filter into screw-top beer or cider bottles. The beer will be ready to use after another 48 hours.

Treacle Ale

1 lb GOLDEN SYRUP
8 oz BLACK TREACLE
8 PINTS WATER
1 oz FRESH YEAST
½ oz GROUND GINGER
RIND OF 1 LEMON

1 · Put the syrup and treacle in a large bowl and cover with boiling water. Stir well until the syrup and treacle have melted.
2 · Add the ginger and thinly peeled lemon rind.
3 · Cool to lukewarm and add the crumbled yeast.

4 · Cover the bowl with a thick cloth and keep in a warm room for three days.
5 · Very carefully syphon off the liquid into bottles without disturbing the yeast sediment.
6 · Cork lightly and keep for a week before drinking.

This was always a very popular harvest drink to accompany "elevenses" and "fourses" cakes, and the midday snack.

In the days before radio and television, evenings were spent round the fire, talking, telling stories and sipping home-made drinks:

> "The christening party drew into a circle round the fire and the men drank beer, heated by thrusting down into the hot coals the point of the long, conical vessel there known as a hooter, while the women and girls sipped elderberry wine and ate hot roasted chestnuts."
>
> —— *Still Glides the Stream*, Chapter 3

Wines and beers may still be warmed in the traditional manner if they are placed in pottery mugs and a hot poker is thrust into them. Lacking open fires, or perhaps for safety reasons, many people prefer to heat the liquid gently in a saucepan, without boiling. A hint of spice or a dash of brandy, or slices of orange or lemon may be added to the hot drink, known as "mulled" wine or beer, which makes a wonderful nightcap to ensure sound sleep.

No cultivated or wild fruits were wasted, and those which were not turned into jams or jellies would surely find their way into a wine or a more expensive but delicious liqueur:

> "One October Saturday afternoon Charity had gone to the more distant Waterside fields to pick sloes, or slans, as the fruit was called locally, intending, when she had filled her basket, to call at the farm. It had been a good year for sloes; never had the bushes been so loaded or the fruit larger and juicier, each sloe like a small plum, misted with pale purple bloom. Her mother had already filled a nine-gallon cask with the wine she had made, but this she had determined to keep for some special occasion, as it had been a kind of vintage year. 'Not a tap shall be knocked into that barrel till the day of Charity's wedding, or the day she gets her own school,' she had declared. But now she had said that if Charity would go round the hedgerows and fill the basket she gave her she would make another quart or

two for what she called common use. 'It's a bit late for them, I know,' she said, 'but there must be pecks still hanging on the boughs, and the wine won't be any the worse for a touch of frost. Better, according to some folks' opinion. 'Twas always said when I was a child that celery, sloes and savoy cabbages wasn't worth a tinker's cuss till they'd been frosted.' And Charity had taken the basket and strolled along the hedgerows, picking the finest."

—— *Still Glides the Stream*, Chapter 10

Liqueur-making is much easier than wine-making or brewing, because there are fewer ingredients, no problems with temperature-taking, and no mess. The fruit is merely soaked in spirit in a screw-top jar in a cool, dark place so that colour is retained. During storage, it is usual to shake the jar from time to time to distribute the ingredients evenly. After a period of infusion, the liquid is filtered through a funnel lined with a coffee filter paper into bottles, sealed firmly and labelled.

Liqueurs develop flavour and smoothness during storage, and they will certainly taste excellent if stored for at least a year. They are delicious on their own, but were often diluted with soda water or clear sparkling lemonade as long summer drinks. In the winter, the rum-, brandy- and whisky-based varieties may be taken with boiling water as a nightcap or cold-soother.

Sloe Gin

1 lb RIPE SLOES
12 oz SUGAR
1½ PINTS GIN

Sloes grow wild, and are like small, hard dark plums. They need to be pricked all over with a darning needle to release their juices.

1 · Wipe the sloes and prick each one.
2 · Place in a large screw-top jar and sprinkle with sugar.
3 · Pour in the gin and seal tightly.

4 · Leave for 12 weeks, shaking the jar occasionally.
5 · Filter into bottles, seal them and label carefully.

Sloe gin is supposed to be at its best after seven years but not many people are strong-minded enough to keep it that long.

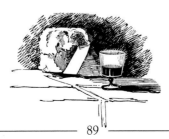

Blackberry Gin

1 lb BLACKBERRIES
4 oz SUGAR
¾ PINT GIN

1 · Use large, ripe, juicy berries, which may be fresh or frozen without sugar. Put fresh or thawed fruit into a screw-top jar and crush the fruit slightly.

2 · Add sugar and gin.
3 · Seal and leave for 3 months, shaking the jar each day for the first 4 weeks.
4 · Filter into bottles, seal and label.

Blackcurrant Brandy

1 lb BLACKCURRANTS
8 oz SUGAR
6 CLOVES
¾ PINT BRANDY

1 · Use large, ripe currants, which may be fresh or frozen without sugar. Top and tail the currants and put into a screw-top jar.
2 · Add sugar, cloves and brandy.

3 · Stir well and seal tightly.
4 · Leave for 3 months, shaking the jar occasionally.
5 · Filter into bottles, seal and label.

Raspberry Brandy

8 oz RASPBERRIES
2 oz SUGAR
1 PINT BRANDY

1 · The berries may be fresh or frozen without sugar. Put into a screw-top jar with the sugar and brandy.

2 · Seal tightly and leave for 4 weeks, shaking the jar occasionally.
3 · Filter into bottles, seal and label.

This is good on its own, but makes an excellent long drink with soda water.

Lemon Rum

1½ LEMONS
ADDITIONAL LEMON JUICE
12 oz SUGAR
¼ PINT WATER
1 PINT DARK RUM

1 · Peel the lemon rind thinly and put into a screw-top jar.
2 · Squeeze out the lemon juice and if necessary add some extra juice to make up to ¼ pint. Put the lemon juice into the jar.
3 · Put the sugar and water into a pan and stir over low heat until the sugar dissolves.

Simmer for 3 minutes and then leave until cold.
4 · Add to the jar with the rum, and seal tightly.
5 · Leave for 4 weeks, shaking the jar occasionally.
6 · Filter into bottles, seal and label.

This is very good on its own, but may be diluted with hot water and drunk as a nightcap or cold cure.

Four Fruit Brandy

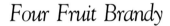

1 lb STRAWBERRIES
1 lb RASPBERRIES
1 lb BLACK CHERRIES
4 oz BLACKCURRANTS
LIGHT SOFT BROWN SUGAR
BRANDY

1 · Put the strawberries and raspberries into a large saucepan.
2 · Stone the cherries and add to the pan with the blackcurrants.
3 · Cover with a lid and simmer together until the juice runs freely.
4 · Strain through a jelly bag without pressure so that the juice remains clear.

5 · For each pint juice, allow 2 oz sugar and ½ pint brandy. Put the juice, sugar and brandy into a screw-top jar.
6 · Crack a few of the cherry stones and add the kernels to the jar.
7 · Seal tightly and leave for 2 weeks, shaking the jar occasionally.
8 · Filter into bottles, seal and label.

Children were not forgotten, and their soft drinks were also made at home. At harvest time, a jug of lemonade with a sprig of borage was particularly popular.

Fresh Lemonade

4 LEMONS
2 lb SUGAR
1 TEASPOON OIL OF LEMON
2 TEASPOONS TARTARIC ACID
2 PINTS BOILING WATER

1 · Squeeze the lemons over sugar in a large bowl.
2 · Stir in the oil and acid. Pour on the boiling water.
3 · Stir well to dissolve sugar and leave until cold.
4 · Pour into sterilised bottles and seal them tightly.
5 · Store in a cool place.
6 · Dilute with hot or cold water to taste.

Lemon oil has a clear pure flavour and is obtainable from chemists and herbalists.

Marrow Rum

1 LARGE FIRM RIPE MARROW
DEMERARA SUGAR

1 · Use a very firm marrow which is too tough for cooking, or for cutting with a knife. Saw through the stalk end and scoop out the seeds and pulp.
2 · Fill the marrow cavity completely with sugar. Put on the top again, and tape securely in place.
3 · Put the marrow into a bag made of strong cloth and hang it in a cool, dry place.
4 · After 2 weeks, fill the marrow with sugar again, seal the top, and hang it in the cloth bag again.
5 · After 4 weeks, the marrow will begin to drip. Take the marrow from the bag and make a hole where the sugar is beginning to drip.
6 · Put a funnel into a bottle and cover it with muslin. Let the liquid run through this covered funnel.
7 · Cork the bottle lightly as fermentation will soon begin. In a few weeks, when fermentation has ceased, cork firmly. Keep for a year before using.

Blackcurrant Liqueur

3 lb BLACKCURRANTS
3½ PINTS RED WINE
SUGAR

The blackcurrants should be very ripe and the wine should be of good quality.

1 · Crush the blackcurrants in a bowl and pour on the wine. Stir well, cover and leave to stand for 48 hours.
2 · Strain the liquid through a jelly bag or clean tea towel.
3 · Weigh the liquid and allow an equal weight of sugar.
4 · Put into a large saucepan and bring to the boil. Boil for 5 minutes. Cool.
5 · Filter into bottles, seal and label.

This is good on its own, or diluted with water. A tablespoon of this liqueur in a glass of dry white wine is a delicious summer drink.

Sherbet

1 lb CASTER SUGAR
8 oz BICARBONATE OF SODA
8 oz TARTARIC ACID
1 TEASPOON OIL OF LEMON

1 · Put the sugar into a bowl and stir in the oil of lemon, mixing well.
2 · Stir in the soda and acid and mix well.
3 · Put into an airtight bottle and seal tightly, as dampness will spoil the sherbet.
4 · Put 1 tablespoon of powder into a glass of water for a fizzy drink which children love.

Lemon Sherbet

2 lb CASTER SUGAR
½ oz CITRIC ACID POWDER
FEW DROPS OF LEMON ESSENCE
FEW DROPS OF YELLOW FOOD COLOURING

1 · Put the sugar into a liquidiser goblet and blend into fine crystals but not powder.
2 · Add the citric acid powder, lemon essence and colouring, and blend just enough to give an even colour.
3 · Spread on a tray and leave to dry.
4 · Put into a screw-top bottle, seal and label.
5 · To serve as a drink, add 2 teaspoons powder to 1 glass water.

Autumn Apple Refresher

PEELINGS AND CORES FROM 4 lb APPLES
1 LEMON
12 SUGAR CUBES
4 PINTS BOILING WATER

1 · Wash the apples well before peeling and coring them (the apple flesh will be useful for puddings or preserves).
2 · Put the peelings and cores into a bowl and pour on the boiling water.
3 · Rub the sugar cubes over the lemon skin to remove the strongly flavoured zest and put the sugar cubes into the bowl.
4 · Cut the lemon across in thin slices and add to the bowl.
5 · Cover and leave overnight.
6 · Strain and sweeten to taste.

This drink is not for keeping, but it is very thirst-quenching and is a good way of using surplus peels and cores which would otherwise be wasted.

Quick Ginger Beer

1 oz ROOT GINGER
1 lb SUGAR
1 oz CREAM OF TARTAR
1 LEMON
8 PINTS BOILING WATER
1 oz FRESH YEAST OR ½ oz DRIED YEAST

1 · Put the ginger into a piece of clean cloth and hit it with a hammer or heavy weight until the ginger is bruised.
2 · Put into a bowl and add the sugar and cream of tartar.
3 · Grate the lemon rind and squeeze out the juice and add to the bowl.
4 · Pour in the boiling water, stir well and leave until cold.
5 · Mix the yeast with 5 tablespoons luke-warm water and add to the bowl.
6 · Cover and leave overnight. Strain through a muslin cloth and bottle into strong screw-top bottles (e.g. those used for cider or beer). Leave for 48 hours before using.

The Ginger Beer Plant

This method provides a permanent source of ginger beer. The solids which result after straining off liquid are the "plant" which should be divided in half before the process is repeated. The "plant" will continue to multiply and may be given away to friends.

To start the plant mix ½ oz fresh yeast or ¼ oz dried yeast with 2 teaspoons ground ginger, 2 teaspoons sugar and ¾ pint water. Leave for 24 hours, and then feed daily with 1 teaspoon ground ginger and 1 teaspoon sugar.

After 7 days strain through a cloth, retaining the liquid. The remaining solid is the plant which should be mixed with ¾ pint water and then fed with ginger and sugar to produce a new batch of ginger beer. The "plant" should be divided in half about every two weeks.

To finish the ginger beer mix the strained liquid with 5 pints cold water, the juice of 2 lemons and 1½ lb sugar which has been dissolved in 2 pints hot water. Mix well and pour into screw-top (beer or cider) bottles. Leave for 1 week before using.

Those who had access to supplies of soft fruit liked to prepare syrups or a similar preparation called a cordial. These syrups were used to flavour dishes, or were diluted with hot or cold water to make refreshing drinks. A spoonful of syrup was used to soothe sore throats or coughs, or was taken in hot water as a nightcap for the same purpose.

"Then she crossed the room to the corner cupboard and reached down from a shelf a half-pint bottle of the raspberry vinegar. 'Slip this in your satchel,' she said. 'You'll find a sip or two comforting when your cough bothers you, and you needn't be afraid to take it. Dr. Fisher won't mind. I send him a pint bottle for his own use every year; though, would you believe it, he has it on his suet puddings. Says it won't keep till he gets his winter touches of bronchitis.'"

——— *Still Glides the Stream*, Chapter 8

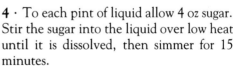

Raspberry Vinegar

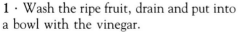

1 PINT RED OR WHITE WINE VINEGAR
1 lb RASPBERRIES
SUGAR

1 · Wash the ripe fruit, drain and put into a bowl with the vinegar.
2 · Cover with a cloth and leave to stand for 4 days, stirring and pressing the fruit occasionally.
3 · Strain through a nylon sieve or jelly bag, pressing the fruit very lightly to extract the juice.

4 · To each pint of liquid allow 4 oz sugar. Stir the sugar into the liquid over low heat until it is dissolved, then simmer for 15 minutes.
5 · Strain into small preserving jars or screw-top bottles and seal firmly.
6 · Dilute with cold water for a refreshing drink, or with hot water for a soothing one.

This is also a good sauce for ice creams or hot steamed puddings.

Blackberry Cordial

2 lb RIPE BLACKBERRIES
1 PINT WHITE VINEGAR
1 lb CUBE SUGAR
8 oz HONEY

The blackberries should be large, ripe and glossy. In the country, it is said that they should never be picked after the end of September as later fruit is spat on by the Devil.

1 · Wash the berries and drain them very thoroughly, and then pat them dry with kitchen paper or a cloth.
2 · Put into a non-metallic bowl and pour over the vinegar. Leave to stand for a week in a cool place, covered with a teacloth. Stir and squeeze the berries two or three times each day to press out the juices.

3 · Strain the liquid into a saucepan, pressing the fruit to extract as much juice as possible.
4 · Add the sugar and honey and boil for 5 minutes.
5 · Cool completely and pour into dark glass bottles.
6 · Cork well and store in a cool place.

Add 1 tablespoon of this cordial to a mug of hot water as a soothing cough and cold reliever, or just as a pleasant bedtime drink.

Winter Cordial

8 oz STONED RAISINS
2 CLOVES
PINCH OF GROUND NUTMEG
1 ORANGE
2 oz CUBE SUGAR
1 PINT BRANDY

The raisins should be large old-fashioned ones which have a rich flavour. The stones may be removed with the point of a knife.

1 · Stone the raisins and put them in a screw-top jar with the cloves and nutmeg.
2 · Rub the sugar cubes over the skin of the orange so that they absorb the richly-coloured and flavoured orange zest.

3 · Add these sugar cubes to the raisins and pour in the brandy.
4 · Seal tightly and leave for 4 weeks.
5 · Filter into bottles, seal and label.

This makes a delicious winter nightcap for a cold evening.

Autumn Cordial

2 lb DAMSONS
1 lb RIPE ELDERBERRIES
2 PINTS WATER
4 lb SUGAR
5 DROPS OIL OF CLOVES
1 TABLESPOON CLEAR HONEY

1 · Halve the damsons and remove their stones.
2 · Crack 12 stones and add them to the damsons.
3 · Pour over the water and leave to stand for 24 hours.
4 · Boil for 15 minutes and strain the liquid over the elderberries, pressing out all the juices from the damsons.
5 · Leave to stand for 24 hours, crushing the berries with a wooden spoon two or three times.
6 · Bring to the boil and then simmer for 5 minutes.
7 · Strain into a clean pan and stir in the sugar.
8 · Heat gently until the sugar has dissolved and then simmer for 10 minutes.
9 · Remove from the heat and stir in the oil of cloves.
10 · Leave until cold and then bottle, adding 1 teaspoon honey to each pint.

Use for a cold, diluted with hot water. Oil of cloves may be obtained from any chemist, but ½ teaspoon ground cloves may be used instead.

Honey Mint Syrup

8 oz HONEY
½ PINT WATER
¼ PINT LEMON JUICE
6 TABLESPOONS FRESH MINT LEAVES

1 · Put the honey, water and lemon juice into a saucepan.
2 · Chop the mint finely and add it to the saucepan.
3 · Bring to the boil and simmer gently for 10 minutes.
4 · Strain and cool, and pour into a screw-top bottle.
5 · Store in the refrigerator.
6 · Dilute to taste with iced water.

Sweetmeats

"At the beginning of the 'eighties the outside world remembered Fordlow Feast to the extent of sending one old woman with a gingerbread stall. On it were gingerbread babies with currants for eyes, brown-and-white striped peppermint humbugs, sticks of pink-and-white rock, and a few boxes and bottles of other sweets. Even there, on that little old stall with its canvas awning, the first sign of changing taste might have been seen, for, one year, side by side with the gingerbread babies stood a box filled with thin, dark brown slabs packed in pink paper. 'What is that brown sweet?' asked Laura, spelling out the word 'Chocolate'. A visiting cousin, being fairly well educated and a great reader, already knew it by name. 'Oh, that's chocolate,' he said off-handedly. 'But don't buy any; it's for drinking. They have it for breakfast in France.' A year or two later, chocolate was a favourite sweet even in a place as remote as the hamlet, but it could no longer be bought from the gingerbread stall, for the old woman no longer brought it to the Feast. Perhaps she had died."

——— *Lark Rise*, Chapter 15

Commercially made sweets were completely unknown a hundred years ago, and the sweet "trade" consisted mainly of old ladies who prepared everything in their own kitchens and sold their confectionery from market or fair stalls or from their own cottage front rooms. Chocolate was very expensive and bitter, and made into drinks by scraping finely and simmering in water for hours to make a thick paste which was then diluted by more water and milk. Eating chocolate was unknown and the favourite sweets were mainly boiled sugar mixtures.

"An old dame sold penny plates of cooked prunes and rice to the village boys in the evening. She also made what was known as sticky toffee, so soft it could be pulled out in lengths, like elastic. She took snuff so freely that no one over twelve years of age would eat this."

——— *Candleford Green*, Chapter 5

Pulled Treacle Toffee

1 lb GRANULATED SUGAR
1 lb BLACK TREACLE
1 oz BUTTER
1 TABLESPOON VINEGAR

1 · Put the sugar, treacle and butter into a thick saucepan and heat very gently until the sugar has melted.
2 · Stir until boiling and then cook to hard ball stage (i.e. when a little of the mixture dropped in cold water forms a hard ball – temperature 247°F/119°C).
3 · Remove the pan from the heat and stir in the vinegar.
4 · Pour into a lightly greased tin and leave until cool enough to handle.
5 · Oil the hands and take a piece of toffee. Pull rapidly with both hands until it is too hard to work any longer, then twist it and cut into pieces with oiled scissors.

Hardbake

1 lb CUBE SUGAR
1 TEASPOON CREAM OF TARTAR
½ PINT WATER
4 oz BLANCHED ALMONDS

1 · Stir the sugar, cream of tartar and water in a heavy saucepan.
2 · Heat gently until the sugar has dissolved.
3 · Boil to hard crack stage (i.e. when a little of the mixture dropped in cold water separates into threads which are hard and brittle – temperature 310°F/154°C).
4 · Stir in the almonds and pour into a greased tin. Break into pieces when cold.

Bonfire Toffee

12 oz DARK SOFT BROWN SUGAR
2 oz BUTTER
1 TABLESPOON VINEGAR
2 TABLESPOONS BOILING WATER
PINCH OF SALT

1 · Put all the ingredients into a large pan and bring to the boil.
2 · Boil to hard crack stage (i.e. when a little of the mixture dropped in cold water separates into threads which are hard and brittle, and a thin piece snaps easily).
3 · Pour into a buttered tin about 8×14 in.
4 · Cool slightly and mark into squares.
5 · When cold, turn out and break into pieces, and store in an airtight tin.

This was a special treat on Bonfire Night, eaten round a big fire in the open air.

Butterscotch

6 oz BUTTER
1 lb LIGHT SOFT BROWN SUGAR
8 oz GOLDEN SYRUP
1 TABLESPOON WATER
PINCH OF CREAM OF TARTAR
½ TEASPOON VANILLA ESSENCE
½ TEASPOON LEMON ESSENCE

1 · Melt the butter in a heavy saucepan and stir in the sugar, syrup and water.
2 · Heat gently until the sugar dissolves.
3 · Bring to the boil and add the cream of tartar.
4 · Boil to soft crack stage (i.e. when a little of the mixture dropped in cold water separates into threads which are hard but not brittle – temperature 280°F/140°C).
5 · Stir in the essences and pour into a greased tin.
6 · When the toffee has cooled a little, mark into squares. Break into pieces when cold.

Honeycomb Toffee

6 oz GRANULATED SUGAR
2 TABLESPOONS HONEY
2 TABLESPOONS GOLDEN SYRUP
2 TABLESPOONS WATER
1½ TEASPOONS BICARBONATE OF SODA

1 · Put the sugar, honey, syrup and water in a heavy pan and heat gently, stirring occasionally, until the sugar has dissolved.
2 · Bring to the boil, then reduce the heat and cook to hard crack stage (i.e. when a little of the mixture dropped in cold water separates into threads which are hard and brittle – temperature 310°F/154°C).
3 · Take off the heat and stir in the bicarbonate of soda.
4 · Pour into a greased tin and leave until cold before breaking into pieces.

The toffee will froth up when the soda is added and form a honeycomb.

Barley Sugar

1 lb GRANULATED SUGAR
¼ PINT WATER
¼ TEASPOON CREAM OF TARTAR
1 TABLESPOON WATER
1 TABLESPOON GOLDEN SYRUP
2 TEASPOONS LEMON ESSENCE

1 · Put the sugar and water in a pan and heat gently until the sugar has dissolved.
2 · Strain and mix in the cream of tartar dissolved in 1 tablespoon water, and the golden syrup.
3 · Boil to hard ball stage (i.e. when a little of the mixture dropped in cold water forms a firm ball which holds its shape, but is still plastic – temperature 247°F/119°C).
4 · Lower the heat and boil gently to hard crack stage (i.e. when a little of the mixture dropped in cold water separates into threads which are hard and brittle – temperature 310°F/154°C).
5 · Take off the heat and immediately put the bottom of the pan in a bowl of cold water for 5 seconds to cool the contents.
6 · Stir in the lemon essence.
7 · Pour on to an oiled slab or tin.
8 · When the mixture is firm, cut in strips, twist and put on a cool part of the oiled surface to get cold.
9 · Wrap in waxed paper or Cellophane and store in screw-top jars.

Toffee Apples

8 SMALL RED APPLES
1 lb DEMERARA SUGAR
⅓ PINT WATER
3 oz BUTTER
2 TEASPOONS POWDERED GLUCOSE

1 · Remove the stalks of the apples and insert a stick in each stalk end.
2 · Put the sugar and water into a thick pan and heat slowly until the sugar dissolves.
3 · Add the butter and glucose and boil to soft crack stage (i.e. when a little of the mixture dropped in cold water separates into threads which are hard but not brittle – temperature 280°F/140°C).
4 · Dip in the apples and put the sticks in a jam jar until the toffee has set hard.
5 · Heat the toffee again and dip in the apples a second time.
6 · Leave the toffee apples in the jar until they are cold and then wrap in waxed paper.

Carrot Ginger Candy

lb CARROTS
1 lb SUGAR
4 TABLESPOONS LEMON JUICE
1½ TEASPOONS GROUND GINGER
6 oz CHOPPED WALNUTS
CASTER SUGAR

1 · Wash and scrape the carrots.

2 · Grate them finely into a saucepan and stir in the sugar.

3 · Cook very gently over low heat, stirring often.

4 · When the sugar has dissolved, add the lemon juice and ginger. Continue cooking and stirring over low heat until all moisture has evaporated and the mixture is thick.

5 · Stir in the nuts.

6 · Sprinkle a flat surface with caster sugar and spread the mixture on this, about ½ in. thick. Sprinkle with a little more sugar.

7 · Leave until cool and mark into squares with a knife. When cold and hard, break into squares.

Root vegetables, particularly carrots, parsnips and beetroot, were traditionally used to give sweetness and bulk to dishes, and carrots are still used in cakes and puddings.

More delicate spiced sweets were relics of an earlier age, and much enjoyed by old ladies, who said that they helped to digest a meal.

Caraway Comfits

1 lb CUBE SUGAR
4 fl oz WATER
8 oz CARAWAY SEEDS
FLOUR
FEW DROPS OF COCHINEAL

1 · Put the sugar and water into a pan and leave to stand for 10 minutes.

2 · Put on low heat and bring to boil, and then boil to hard ball stage (i.e. when a little of the mixture dropped in cold water can be formed into a firm ball – temperature 247°F/119°C).

3 · Drop in the caraway seeds and stir them well till coated with the sugar syrup.

4 · Lift them out and place on a sieve with a very light sprinkling of flour. Shake well to separate the seeds and leave to dry.

5 · Bring the syrup to the boil again, add seeds, stir well and return to sieve.

6 · Leave to dry and then repeat the process several times until the sugar-coated seeds are the required size – they are best if made the size of a small pea.

7 · Some may be tinted pink with a little cochineal in the final boiling.

8 · Store in an airtight tin and use as sweets or as cake decorations.

Cinnamon Drops

1 lb GRANULATED SUGAR
1 oz GROUND CINNAMON
½ PINT WATER
2 EGG WHITES

1 · Stir the sugar and cinnamon together until evenly coloured.
2 · Stir in the water until evenly mixed.
3 · Whisk the egg whites to stiff peaks and fold into the sugar mixture.
4 · Line a baking sheet with non-stick baking parchment. Put on the sugar mixture in teaspoonsful.
5 · Put into a very low oven (250°F/120°C/ Gas Mark ½) and leave to dry out for 3 hours.
6 · Store in an airtight tin.

"Every autumn, the dealer came to purchase the produce of her beehives. Then, in her pantry doorway, a large muslin bag was suspended to drain the honey from the broken pieces of comb into a large, red pan which stood beneath, while, on her doorstep, the end house children waited to see 'the honeyman' carry out and weigh the whole combs. One year – one never-to-be-forgotten year – he had handed to each of them a rich, dripping fragment of comb. He never did it again; but they always waited, for the hope was almost as sweet as the honey."

—— *Lark Rise*, Chapter 5

Honey Puff

3 TABLESPOONS HONEY
5 TABLESPOONS GRANULATED SUGAR
4 TABLESPOONS WATER
½ oz BUTTER
½ TEASPOON MALT VINEGAR
½ TEASPOON BICARBONATE OF SODA

1 · Put the honey, sugar, water, butter and vinegar into a saucepan and heat slowly, stirring until the sugar has dissolved and the butter melted.
2 · Bring to the boil, cover and boil for 2 minutes.
3 · Uncover and boil without stirring for 5 minutes.
4 · Take off the heat, stir in the bicarbonate of soda and pour into a small greased tin.
5 · Leave until cold and set before breaking into pieces.
6 · Eat up quickly as this sweetmeat gets very sticky.

Honey Toffee

10 oz BUTTER
4 oz HONEY
¼ PINT WATER

1 · Put all the ingredients into a heavy pan and heat gently until the butter has melted.
2 · Boil to soft ball stage (i.e. when a little of the mixture dropped in cold water can be formed into a soft ball when rolled in the fingers – temperature 237°F/114°C).
3 · Pour into a greased tin and leave until cool.
4 · Mark in small pieces and break up.
5 · Wrap each piece in waxed paper.

Honey Kisses

1 oz CANDIED PEEL
2½ oz BLANCHED ALMONDS
2 TEASPOONS CLEAR HONEY
ICING SUGAR

1 · Chop the peel very finely and grate the almonds.
2 · Mix the peel and almonds together and stir in the honey.
3 · Form into small balls and roll them in icing sugar.
4 · Leave to dry for 24 hours.

Laura thought that Miss Lane's laboriously made wine jelly was not nearly as nice as her favourite red jujubes, and these soft sweets were always popular with young children.

Apricot Jujubes

1 lb DRIED APRICOTS
2¼ lb GRANULATED SUGAR
ICING SUGAR

1 · Soak the apricots in water to cover for 24 hours.
2 · Drain well and put through the fine screen of a mincing machine, or chop finely in a food processor.
3 · Put into a saucepan with the sugar. Cook gently for 1 hour, stirring often to prevent sticking.
4 · Rinse a shallow tin with cold water, and pour in the apricot mixture.
5 · When cold, cut into small pieces and roll them in icing sugar.

Fresh Fruit Jellies

¼ PINT UNSWEETENED FRUIT JUICE
3 oz GRANULATED SUGAR
3 oz POWDERED GLUCOSE
1 oz GELATINE
CASTER SUGAR

Fresh, canned, bottled or boxed fruit juice may be used. Lemon, orange, blackcurrant, apple and pineapple are all good flavours for this purpose.

1 · Put the juice into a saucepan with the sugar and stir over low heat until dissolved.
2 · Add the glucose and gelatine and heat gently until the gelatine has melted.
3 · Rinse a 6 in. tin in cold water and pour in the fruit mixture.
4 · Leave until cold and firmly set.

5 · Dip the tin into hot water for a second and turn out on to a flat surface.
6 · Cut into cubes and coat with caster sugar.
7 · A little food colouring may be added to make the jellies more attractive. Eat the jellies freshly made.

Fairs and feast days were an important part of the country calendar, and brightly coloured sweets caught the revellers' eyes and were often taken home as tokens for those who had been unable to join the merry party.

Candied Roses and Violets

1 TEACUP SMALL ROSEBUDS OR 2 TEACUPS VIOLETS
4 fl oz WATER
8 oz GRANULATED SUGAR

1 · Gather the flowers in the early morning just when the dew has dried, and remove any stems. Wash gently in cold water and drain in a colander without bruising them.
2 · Put the water into a heavy pan and bring to the boil.
3 · Take off the heat and stir in the sugar until dissolved.
4 · Return to the heat and stir in the flowers. Simmer gently to soft ball stage (i.e. when a little of the syrup dropped in cold

water can be formed into a soft ball when rolled in the fingers – temperature 237°F/114°C).
5 · Take off the heat and stir until the syrup begins to granulate and looks like coarse oatmeal.
6 · Pour into a colander and shake as the flowers cool so that any spare sugar is shaken off them.
7 · When cold, store in screw-top jars. Use as sweetmeats or cake decorations.

Easy Candied Peel

8 oz ORANGE AND LEMON PEEL
1 lb SUGAR
½ PINT WATER

1 · Scrape white pith from the pieces of peel and cut the peel into large neat pieces.
2 · Put into a pan, cover with water, and boil until the peel is soft. Drain well.
3 · Stir the sugar and water together and heat gently to boiling point.
4 · Continue boiling to soft ball stage (i.e. a little dropped in cold water will form a soft ball – temperature 237°F/114°C).
5 · Add the peel and simmer for 10 minutes.
6 · Drain and place on a wire rack.
7 · Sprinkle with sugar and leave to dry.

Quince Leather

2 lb QUINCES
¼ PINT WATER
SUGAR
ICING SUGAR

1 · Wash and wipe the quinces but do not peel or core them.
2 · Cut the fruit into small pieces and put into a pan with the water.
3 · Simmer very gently until the fruit is very soft. Put through a sieve and weigh the pulp. Put into a very thick pan with an equal amount of sugar.
4 · Stir over low heat until the mixture dries and leaves the sides of the pan clear.
5 · Pour into shallow dishes lined with foil (toffee tins or ice-cube trays are the right depth) and leave in a warm place to dry for 2-3 days. A warm airing cupboard or a rack over a cooker is a good place to keep the mixture as it dries.
6 · Cut into strips and then squares and dust with icing sugar.
7 · Store between layers of waxed or greaseproof paper in tins or airtight boxes.

This is a very old way of preserving fruit and makes a delicious sweetmeat which is eaten on its own or with cheese. Apple leather and pear leather may be made in the same way.

Home and Beauty

"When I am old,
Give me for heaven a little house set on a heath,
The blue hills behind; the blue sea before.
The brick floors scoured crimson, the flagstones like snow;
The brass taps and candlesticks like gold,
And there, in my soft grey gown between the holly-hocks,
Upon a day of days I would welcome an old poet;
And pour him tea, and walk on the heath, and talk the sun down;
And then by the wood fire he should read me the poems of his passionate youth,
And make new ones praising friendship above love!"

——— *Country Calendar,* The Earthly Paradise

Country women were proud of their houses, and however poor and small the dwellings were, they were kept sparkling clean and shining. This could be a difficult day-long task, for shops could not provide patent cleaning materials, but only the oils, fats, colourings and basic chemicals from which they had to be made. Polishes, soaps, air fresheners and beauty preparations were made by housewives from these raw materials amplified with home-grown herbs, flowers, vegetables and fruit to make the original versions of so many necessities which are taken for granted today. Housekeeping therefore became a double labour, not only absorbing a lot of time and physical effort, but also requiring forethought and additional time for making the necessary equipment.

No old-fashioned housewife would think of whisking through a room once a week, but would make cleaning and laundering the centre of her life:

"It was a pleasant home, though bare, for Queenie kept it spotless, scrubbing her deal table and whitening her floor with hearthstone every morning and keeping the two brass candlesticks on her mantelpiece polished till they looked like gold."

——— *Lark Rise,* Chapter 5

"Every morning, as soon as the men had been packed off to work, the older children to school, the smaller ones to play, and the baby had been bathed and put to sleep in its cradle, rugs and mats were carried out of doors and banged against walls, fireplaces were 'ridded up' [riddled] and tables and floors were scrubbed. In wet weather, before scrubbing, the stone floor had often to be scraped with an old knife-blade to loosen the trodden-in mud; for, although there was a scraper for shoes beside every doorstep, some of the stiff, clayey mud would stick to the insteps and uppers of boots. . . .

The morning cleaning proceeded to the accompaniment of neighbourly greetings and shouting across garden and fences, for the first sound of the banging of mats was a signal for others to bring out theirs, and it would be 'Have 'ee heard this?' and 'What d'ye think of that?' until industrious housewives declared that they would take to banging their mats overnight, for they never knew if it was going to take them two minutes or two hours."

—— *Lark Rise*, Chapter 6

Beeswax Polish

PURE BEESWAX
PURE TURPENTINE
FEW DROPS OF POT POURRI OIL

Beeswax may be obtained from bee-keeping organisations (often on display at county shows) and from the National Trust. It is most important to use pure turpentine.

1 · Shred the beeswax with a cheese grater into a screw-top jar.
2 · Cover with turpentine and leave for at least 2 weeks, stirring occasionally. The finished polish should be a smooth paste, but a little more turpentine may be needed from time to time.
3 · A few drops of essential oil, such as pot pourri oil, lavender or rosemary, may be added when the polish is ready.

Household washing presented big problems when few houses had running water:

"Monday was washing-day, and then the place fairly hummed with activity. 'What d'ye think of the weather?' 'Shall we get 'em dry?' were the questions shouted across gardens, or asked as the women met going to and from the well for water. There was no gossiping at corners that morning. It was before the days of patent soaps and washing powders, and much hard rubbing was involved. There were no washing coppers, and the clothes had to be boiled in the big cooking pots over the fire. Often these inadequate vessels would boil over and fill the house with ashes and steam. The small children would hang round their mothers' skirts and hinder them, and tempers grew short and nerves frayed long before the clothes, well blued, were hung on the lines or spread on the hedges. In wet weather they had to be dried indoors, and no one who has not experienced it can imagine the misery of living for several days with a firmament of drying clothes on lines overhead."

—— *Lark Rise*, Chapter 6

Looking After Lace

A few drops of coffee added to rinsing water will give it a creamy tint. Starch should never be used for fine lace, but a little borax dissolved in the rinsing water will give the desired stiffness. The water in which rice has been cooked is also good for giving a light stiffness.

To iron lace, put it on a blanket with the wrong side uppermost and put a cloth over the top. Iron carefully, and lift any raised flowers gently with the fingers.

Embroidery Care

If there is any idea that colours may run, do not wash embroidery in soap or detergent. Instead prepare two bowls of bran water by immersing 1 lb rough bran tied in a cloth bag in each bowl and filling them with warm water. Put the embroidery into one bowl and press gently until the water is dirty. Repeat in the other bowl. If the embroidery is very dirty, make up more bran water, using the same bran bags. Rinse in cold water, squeezing out as much water as possible, and hang to dry. When nearly dry, iron quickly on the wrong side.

In spite of hard work and poverty, women took every chance to keep themselves attractive, and although baths were infrequent because of water shortage, they were very thorough. Miss Lane, the postmistress of Candleford Green, was an elegant lady who took what she called her "canary dip" in a shallow, saucer-shaped bath in her bedroom in a few inches of warm rain water well laced with eau-de-cologne. She only bathed once a week, and in winter the bath was placed by her bedroom fire, but there was a screen at all seasons to keep off draughts. On farm churning days, a quart of buttermilk was delivered for cleaning her face and hands.

Her maid Zillah only washed herself all over in a basin, while the blacksmiths took baths on Wednesdays and Saturdays in Miss Lane's converted brewhouse. Laura also used the brewhouse on Friday nights, the water being drawn from a pump in the yard, through a hose-pipe into the old brewing copper. The smiths used a long deep zinc bath, but Laura and any visitors used a hip-bath standing on a square of matting. This made a pleasant contrast to her home at Lark Rise, where all the water came from the well and had to be boiled in a cauldron over the fire.

Rain water was a precious commodity in the household, much used for washing and cleaning:

"Against the wall of every well-kept cottage stood a tarred or green-painted water butt to catch and store the rain-water from the roof. This saved many journeys to the well with buckets, as it could be used for cleaning and washing clothes and for watering small, precious things in the garden. It was also valued for toilet purposes and the women would hoard the last drops for themselves and their children to wash in. Rain-water was supposed to be good for the complexion, and, though they had no money to spend upon beautifying themselves, they were not too far gone in poverty to neglect such means as they had to that end."

—— *Lark Rise*, Chapter 1

Relaxing Bath Herbs

MINT
THYME
SAGE
ROSEMARY
LEMON BALM
LEMON VERBENA
LAVENDER FLOWERS
CAMOMILE FLOWERS

1 · Make a mixture of some or all of the herbs.
2 · Make muslin bags (the size of a lavender bag) and fill with the herbs.

3 · Put a herb bag into the bath as the warm water runs, and discard after use. The herbs provide a relaxant for tired muscles.

Herbal Hair Tonic

4 TABLESPOONS ROSEMARY OR SAGE
½ PINT CIDER VINEGAR
½ PINT WATER

1 · Put the herbs into a saucepan and cover with the vinegar and water.
2 · Bring to the boil and then simmer for 5 minutes. Cool, strain and bottle.
3 · Apply a few drops of the tonic to the scalp daily with cotton wool.

Sage is a tonic for the hair, while rosemary promotes growth.

Marigold Skin Cleanser

2 TABLESPOONS MARIGOLD PETALS
½ PINT BOILING WATER

1 · Put the marigold petals into a small pan. Add the boiling water and gently simmer for 5 minutes.

2 · Cool, strain and bottle.

This cleanser will keep for a week in the refrigerator. Rub into the skin to act as a skin tonic, softener and moisturiser.

Skin Tonic

2 fl oz WITCH HAZEL
1 fl oz ROSEWATER
1 fl oz ORANGE FLOWER WATER

1 · Mix together and keep in a screw-top jar or bottle.

2 · Apply with cotton wool to cleanse and refresh the skin.

Eye Soothers

To soothe and smooth the wrinkled skin round eyes, put freshly grated raw potatoes into a gauze pad and put this over the closed eyes for 10 minutes.

Make up some strong camomile tea with camomile flowers, and wring out cotton wool pads in the tea. Put over closed eyes for 10 minutes.

Thin slices of cucumber placed over the eyes will cool and soothe.

Beautiful Vegetables

Fresh vegetables are not only delicious but often have health-giving effects. They are always best freshly cut rather than stored.

Carrots and parsnips have a whitening effect on the skin, and may be eaten raw or cooked.

Spinach and onions purify the blood and an old saying is "an onion a day keeps the doctor away".

Lettuce and watercress supply iron to the blood and give colour to the cheeks. The stalk of the lettuce aids sleep, and a lettuce sandwich made with brown bread and butter aids insomniacs.

Parsley aids digestion and gives a clear skin, so the garnish on the sandwiches is worth eating. It also takes away the after-effects of onions and garlic on the breath.

Women were not allowed to work in the vegetable gardens or allotments, as this was considered to be "men's work", and it was considered unwomanly to work outside the home. They were however allowed to cultivate a flower garden, and used the flowers for scented preparations which made their houses smell delicious:

> "They grew all the sweet old-fashioned cottage garden flowers, pinks and sweet williams and love-in-a-mist, wallflowers and forget-me-nots in spring and hollyhocks and Michaelmas daisies in autumn. Then there were lavender and sweetbriar bushes, and southern-wood, sometimes called 'lad's love', but known there as 'old man'.
>
> —— *Lark Rise*, Chapter 6

Lavender Bottles

These bundles of lavender plaited with narrow ribbon were used to mark dozens and half-dozens in a linen chest or cupboard. The lavender must be picked when in full flower on long stems which are still supple, and the lavender must be used immediately as the stalks become brittle after an hour or two. Take 22 stalks, and a piece of narrow baby ribbon about 2 ft long. Tie the stems firmly together with one end of the ribbon immediately below the flower heads.

Turn the bunch upside down and bend the stalks gently out and downwards over the heads so that the flowers look as if they are in a cage of stems. Space out the stems in pairs and weave the long end of the ribbon under and over the stems until the heads are completely enclosed. The "weaving" should be rather tight at bottom and top and looser in the centre so that the top is bottle-shaped. When the heads are completely covered, wind the long end of the ribbon firmly round the stems and tie firmly in a bow. Leave about 4 ins stalk and trim evenly with scissors. The scent of the "bottles" lasts for years among linen, or tucked into drawers.

> "A blue-and-white dish of oranges stuck with cloves stood upon the dresser. They were dry and withered at that time of the year, but still contributed their quota to the distinctive flavour of the year."
>
> —— *Candleford Green*

To Laura, these looked just like old oranges, but they were in fact pomanders, made since time immemorial to give a long-lasting fresh fragrance to wardrobes and rooms.

Pomanders

ORANGES OR LEMONS
WHOLE CLOVES
GROUND CINNAMON
ORRIS ROOT POWDER

1 · Take thin-skinned oranges or lemons and prick them all over with a fork.
2 · Insert whole cloves into each hole until the whole surface of each fruit is covered with a tiny space between each clove.
3 · Put each fruit on to a piece of tissue paper and sprinkle lightly with ground cinnamon and orris root powder.
4 · Wrap firmly and keep in a warm dry place like an airing-cupboard until the orange or lemon is completely dry.
5 · Arrange in bowls, or tie a piece of ribbon around each one so that it may be hung in a clothes cupboard.

Lark Rise Pot Pourri

1 lb RED ROSE PETALS
4 oz LEMON VERBENA LEAVES
4 oz ROSE GERANIUM LEAVES
4 oz LAVENDER FLOWERS
4 oz ROSEMARY LEAVES
1 TEASPOON MARJORAM
1 TEASPOON LEMON THYME
1 TEASPOON ORRIS ROOT POWDER
1 TEASPOON GROUND ALLSPICE
1 TEASPOON GROUND CLOVES
PINCH OF GROUND NUTMEG
½ TEASPOON DRIED ORANGE PEEL
½ TEASPOON DRIED LEMON PEEL
4 DROPS ROSE OIL
2 DROPS ROSEMARY OIL

Flowers and leaves should be picked on a warm dry day when the plants are in peak condition.

1 · Spread petals and leaves on wire cake racks or newspaper on a table in a shady, dry area of the house. When they are crisp and dry, put into separate containers until you are ready to make the final mixture.
2 · When everything is ready, put the flowers and leaves into a large cake tin or polythene box and add the herbs, orris root, spices, peels and oils.
3 · Keep tightly covered for 6 weeks, stirring occasionally or shaking the box well.
4 · Divide the mixture between individual containers or packets and seal tightly.

Homely Remedies

"They made a good deal of camomile tea, which they drank freely to ward off colds, to soothe the nerves, and as a general tonic. A large jug of this was always prepared and stood ready for heating up after confinements. The horehound was used with honey in a preparation to be taken for sore throats and colds on the chest. Peppermint tea was made rather as a luxury than a medicine; it was brought out on special occasions and drunk from wine-glasses; and the women had a private use for the pennyroyal, though, judging from appearances, it was not very effective."

—— *Lark Rise,* Chapter 6

The village doctor was a wise man who rarely charged his poorer patients, but would raise the prices for his richer ones accordingly. It was mutually accepted, however, that he was only called out in real need when limbs were broken or fevers were violent. There were always one or two local women who assisted at births and looked after the dying, even preparing them for burial. Each housewife took pride in looking after her family's health to the best of her ability, preparing homely remedies in the same way that she filled her larder, preserving seasonal herbs, flowers and berries.

A kind of self-help system operated in every village, with the better-off and professional classes recognising their responsibility for those less fortunate:

"For the sick there were custard puddings, home-made jellies and half-bottles of port, and it was an unwritten law in the parish that, by sending a plate to the vicarage at precisely 1.30 on any Sunday, a convalescent could claim a dinner from the vicarage joint."

—— *Candleford Green,* Chapter 3

Even the poorest women prepared their remedies for homely everyday problems. They knew the properties of both wild and cultivated herbs, and a cup of herb tea soothed many minor ills. Cowslip tea was considered to be a special delicacy, simply as a refreshingly fragrant drink, but other flowers and herbs had more specific uses, soothing away insomnia and indigestion and easing pain. The best way of storing herbal recipes is to keep them in an airtight container, away from the light. They should last from one year till the next.

Camomile Tea

This flower makes a rather bitter tea, but it is an excellent remedy against sleeplessness. The flower heads may be gathered at any time between spring and autumn. Spread them out on paper and dry in a warm room or in the sun. Store in an airtight box or jar. Use two large teaspoons of camomile to a cupful of boiling water and sweeten to taste.

Inhalant for Colds

4 TABLESPOONS PEPPERMINT LEAVES
4 TABLESPOONS LIME FLOWERS
4 TABLESPOONS CAMOMILE FLOWERS
4 TABLESPOONS SAGE LEAVES
2 PINTS BOILING WATER

1 · Shred the peppermint and sage leaves and put into a bowl with lime and camomile flowers.
2 · Pour on the boiling water.
3 · At once, bend your head over the bowl with a towel over your head so that the vapours do not escape, and inhale the steam for 15 minutes.
4 · Go straight to bed or stay indoors for an hour afterwards.

(This recipe is not suitable for anyone suffering from hayfever.)

To Ease Nettle Rash

Rub the rash with a little parsley to soothe the skin.

Wart Remover

Remove beans from broad bean pods and use the inside of the pods to rub the warts.

Teeth Whitener

Rub the teeth with fresh sage leaves.

Headache Relief

Infuse 1 oz rosemary flowers in 1 pint boiling water for 15 minutes. Cool and bottle, after straining. Drink a hot wineglassful four times daily.

Bumps and bruises were another minor hazard relieved by herbs and soothing oils, while abrasions and rashes were easily dealt with by the application of honey.

Bruise Oil

4 TABLESPOONS LEMON BALM
4 TABLESPOONS ROSEMARY
4 TABLESPOONS CAMOMILE FLOWERS
4 TABLESPOONS ROSEBUDS
4 TABLESPOONS SAGE
4 TABLESPOONS LAVENDER FLOWERS
4 TABLESPOONS SOUTHERNWOOD
4 TABLESPOONS WORMWOOD
SALAD OIL

1 · Chop the leaves and flowers finely and place in a bowl.
2 · Cover with salad oil.
3 · Cover and leave to stand for 14 days, stirring often.
4 · Put the mixture into a large saucepan and simmer very gently until the herbs become crisp and their oils have been extracted. The oil should not get hotter than boiling water.
5 · Strain through a filter into a bottle and seal tightly.
6 · Rub the oil gently on the bruised area twice daily.

Honey for Health

Honey was appreciated for its antiseptic qualities, and the country housewife was never without a small pot in the medicine cupboard.

Scalds heal rapidly and the pain will be relieved by the application of a little honey on a clean dressing.

Skin irritations, rashes and itching can be soothed by applying honey, which helps to heal without leaving scars.

Septic wounds may be cleaned and healed if honey is applied gently. A festering wound which is swelling will be eased by honey which draws out the poisons and helps to form new healthy tissues. Deep cuts used to be treated quickly with an application of cobwebs to stop the bleeding, followed by a smear of honey before being tightly bound.

There was no money to spare for patent medicines, ointments or tonics, and the vegetable and herb patch gave speedy answers for everyday problems.

Oxfordshire Specialities

"That afternoon, when Laura arrived, a little round table in the hearthplace had already been laid for tea. And what a meal! There were boiled new-laid eggs and scones and honey and home-made jam, and, to crown all, a dish of fresh Banbury cakes. The carrier had a standing order to bring her a dozen of these cakes every market day.

It seemed a pity to Laura that the first time she had been offered two eggs at one meal she could barely eat one and that the Banbury cake, hitherto to her a delicious rarity only seen in her home when purchased by visiting aunts, should flake and crumble almost untasted upon her plate because she felt too excited and anxious to eat." —— *Candleford Green*, Chapter 1

The Banbury Cake was a speciality of north Oxfordshire, where Flora Thompson spent her childhood, but it was an elaborate cake and too expensive and difficult to make for the cottage-dwellers. The cake had been enjoyed by Oxfordshire people since Elizabethan times, and was praised by many writers, including Ben Jonson. The earliest version of the Banbury Cake consisted of a pastry case around a yeasted currant cake filling, derived from the first Simnel cakes, and rather like a Scots Black Bun. Later it became a yeast pastry cake with a filling of dried fruit, rather like today's Danish pastries, and this version grew in popularity during the eighteenth century, and was the type sold commercially in Banbury. Supplies were sent out to the surrounding countryside, and such a treat was reserved for special occasions. Today's version is more simply made with puff pastry.

 Banbury Cakes

8 oz PUFF PASTRY
1 oz UNSALTED BUTTER
2 TEASPOONS PLAIN FLOUR
1 TABLESPOON DARK RUM
4 oz CURRANTS
1 oz DARK SOFT BROWN SUGAR
1 oz CHOPPED MIXED CANDIED PEEL
1 TEASPOON GROUND CINNAMON
1 TEASPOON GROUND NUTMEG
Glaze
MILK AND CASTER SUGAR

1 · Preheat oven to moderately hot (400°F/200°C/Gas Mark 6).

2 · Roll out the pastry thinly and cut out oval shapes about 6×4 in.

3 · Melt the butter in a small thick pan and take off the heat. Stir in the flour and rum.

4 · Add the currants, sugar, peel and spices and mix well.

5 · Divide the mixture between the pieces of pastry, placing a heap of the fruit in the centre of each.

6 · Fold the long ends of the pastry over the filling so they just overlap. Turn over short ends to enclose the filling.

7 · Turn over the pastry cases and flatten slightly with a rolling pin to give ovals about 4 in. long. Cut three short diagonal slits on top of each one.

8 · Rinse a baking sheet in cold water and place the cakes with the seams downwards.

9 · Brush with a little milk and sprinkle with caster sugar.

10 · Bake for 20 minutes until crisp and golden.

11 · Cool on a wire rack.

12 · Serve freshly baked.

Most of the dishes which are known as county specialities are obviously connected with the Oxford colleges, for they are much too rich or complicated for the country people. A few however derived from the everyday foods like the cottage pig and the local supplies of flour gleaned by the women in the wide clay fields after the harvest.

Oxfordshire Ham Cure

1 lb DARK SOFT BROWN SUGAR
1 lb COOKING SALT
4 oz JUNIPER BERRIES
½ oz SALTPETRE
3 pints BEER
1 LARGE LEG OF FRESH PORK

1 · Put the sugar, salt, berries, saltpetre and beer into a large thick pan and heat gently while the sugar dissolves.

2 · Continue heating gently and bring just to the boil.

3 · Leave until completely cold.

4 · Put the pork in a large bowl into which it just fits.

5 · Pour over the liquid, cover with a cloth and leave in a cold place (the bottom of the refrigerator is very suitable).

6 · Rub the liquid into the pork each day for a week.

7 · Leave for 3 weeks more, rubbing in the liquid three times a week.

8 · Remove from the liquid and wrap in a double layer of muslin. Hang in a cool dry place to dry.

9 · When finished, the ham may be smoked, or may be boiled straight away.

Oxford Sausages

1 lb PORK
1 lb VEAL
1 lb BEEF SUET
8 oz DAY-OLD BREADCRUMBS
¼ pint WATER OR STOCK
GRATED RIND OF 1 LEMON
6 FINELY CHOPPED SAGE LEAVES
1 TEASPOON SALT
1 TEASPOON PEPPER
PINCH OF GROUND NUTMEG
PINCH OF FRESH THYME
PINCH OF FRESH MARJORAM

1 · Mince the pork, veal and suet through the coarse blade of the mincer, or chop in a food processor.

2 · Add breadcrumbs and water or stock.

3 · Stir in the seasonings and herbs. Mix very well and leave to stand for 2 hours in a cool place.

4 · Form into sausage shapes.

It was traditional to fry the sausages in unsalted butter, and sometimes they were dipped in beaten egg and breadcrumbs before cooking.

Oxford Brawn Sauce

Brawn (see Chapter Three) was a favourite dish which might be eaten for breakfast or at teatime. In medieval times, it was eaten "soused" with a vinegar dressing. By the sixteenth century, brawn was being served with mustard as the first course of the main meal. The traditional Oxford Sauce combined the two seasonings, and it is very good with cold meats.

Mix together 1 tablespoon dark soft brown sugar with 1 teaspoon made mustard, a good pinch of salt and a good grinding of black peppercorns. Add 4 tablespoons oil and 2 tablespoons vinegar and mix well.

Oxford Dumplings

4 oz CHEDDAR CHEESE
2 oz BUTTER
2 EGGS
SALT AND PEPPER
4 oz DAY-OLD BREADCRUMBS
1 oz DRIED BREADCRUMBS

1 · Grate the cheese and then beat it into the butter.
2 · Beat in the eggs and season well with salt and pepper.
3 · Add the day-old breadcrumbs to make a stiff mixture.
4 · Form into dumplings and roll in dried breadcrumbs.
5 · Fry in hot deep fat or oil and serve with gravy or tomato sauce.

Banbury Apple Pie

1½ lb COOKING APPLES
4 oz CURRANTS
2 oz CHOPPED MIXED CANDIED PEEL
PINCH OF GROUND GINGER
PINCH OF GROUND CINNAMON
3 oz BUTTER
2 oz LIGHT SOFT BROWN SUGAR
8 oz SHORTCRUST PASTRY
MILK
CASTER SUGAR

1 · Peel, core and slice the apples.
2 · Mix the currants, peel and spices.
3 · Melt the butter.
4 · Put one-third apples into a buttered piedish. Sprinkle on a layer of the currant mixture and then half the butter. Repeat the layers, finishing with apples.
5 · Sprinkle with the sugar and pour in ¼ pint boiling water.
6 · Cover with the pastry and brush lightly with milk.
7 · Bake in a moderate oven (375°F/ 190°C/Gas Mark 5) for 35 minutes.
8 · As soon as the pie comes out of the oven, brush again with milk and sprinkle thickly with caster sugar.

A favourite dish in richer houses belonging to yeoman farmers, the clergy or the professional classes was Oxford Johns made by quickly frying thin slices of fresh mutton or beef in butter with a sprinkling of finely chopped shallots or onions, and a good seasoning of salt, pepper and ground mace. Confusingly, another favourite dish was known by the same name, and was cheap enough to be enjoyed by everyone.

Oxford Johns

4 oz PLAIN FLOUR
½ TEASPOON BAKING POWDER
2 TEASPOONS SUGAR
2 oz LARD
1 oz CURRANTS

1 · Sieve the flour and baking powder together and stir in the sugar.
2 · Rub in the lard until the mixture is like fine breadcrumbs.
3 · Stir in the currants and mix to a stiff dough with a little cold water.
4 · Roll out thinly and cut into 2 in. squares.
5 · Put on a greased baking sheet and bake in a hot oven (400°F/200°C/Gas Mark 6) for 10 minutes.
6 · Cool on a wire rack and eat freshly baked.

Similarly, two dishes are known as Oxford Pudding, one being light and more expensive with eggs and apricots, while the other, given below, is a version of the traditional puddings made with breadcrumbs.

Oxford Crumb Pudding

4 oz BREADCRUMBS OR SPONGECAKE CRUMBS
4 oz SHREDDED SUET
4 oz CURRANTS
2 TABLESPOONS LIGHT SOFT BROWN SUGAR
¼ TEASPOON GROUND NUTMEG
PINCH OF SALT
2 EGG YOLKS

1 · Mix together the crumbs, suet, currants, sugar, nutmeg and salt.
2 · Mix with the egg yolks to make a firm mixture when pressed firmly with the hands.
3 · Shape into balls the size of a bread roll.
4 · Fry in butter until golden brown, shaking the pan all the time so that the puddings remain round.
5 · Serve at once with melted butter and sugar.

Another version of this pudding was made with the addition of candied peel, whole eggs and milk to make a thick creamy consistency. Spoonfuls of the mixture were fried in butter and sprinkled with sugar. This variation was known as New College Pudding, but the other colleges preferred the same mixture boiled as a large pudding.

Oxford Marmalade has become a world-famous preserve since its introduction by the Cooper family. It was much enjoyed by the college men and townsfolk.

Oxford Dark Marmalade

3 lb SEVILLE ORANGES
1 LEMON
5 pints WATER
6 lb SUGAR
1 TABLESPOON BLACK TREACLE

1 · Cut the oranges in half and squeeze the juice into a preserving pan.

2 · Remove the pips, tie them in a muslin bag or piece of cotton, and suspend them in the pan.

3 · Cut the fruit into thick shreds or chunks. Put into the pan with the juice of the lemon and the water. Simmer for 2 hours until the peel is tender.

4 · Remove the bag of pips and squeeze out any liquid back into the pan.

5 · Stir in the sugar and black treacle and heat gently until the sugar has dissolved.

6 · Boil rapidly to setting point which should take 30-40 minutes.

7 · Cool slightly and stir well so that the peel does not form a layer.

8 · Put into hot jars and cover with a waxed paper circle. Either cover at once or leave until completely cold.

This is a richly flavoured dark marmalade; the flavour may be enhanced by adding 4 tablespoons whisky or rum just before potting. It is very important to simmer the peel long enough to soften it completely before the sugar is added, or else the marmalade will become syrupy with hard chunks of peel.

" 'Now, then, all together, boys,' some one would shout, and the company would revert to old favourites. Of these, one was 'The Barleymow'. Trolled out in chorus, the first verse went:

> Oh, when we drink out of our noggins, my boys,
>   We'll drink to the barleymow.
> We'll drink to the barleymow, my boys,
>   We'll drink to the barleymow.
> So knock your pint on the settle's back;
>   Fill again, in again, Hannah Brown,
> We'll drink to the barleymow, my boys,
>   We'll drink now the barley's mown.

So they went on, increasing the measure in each stanza, from noggins to half-pints, pints, quarters, gallons, barrels, hogsheads, brooks, ponds, rivers, seas and oceans. That song could be made to last an whole evening, or it could be dropped as soon as they got tired."

—— *Lark Rise,* Chapter 4

Countrymen were very fond of their drinks, and they gathered in ale-houses to talk and sing and drink their pints. As the agricultural seasons passed, they drank to the success of seed-sowing or harvest, the sowing of beans, the shearing of sheep and the start of ploughing. At home in the evenings, there was no synthetic entertainment and the whole family would sit around the fire, drinking hot beer or wine and chatting amiably. Oxfordshire was particularly famous for its "nightcaps", many of them associated with the college-brewing of ale and with fine imported wines, but the villagers would make do with beer from the ale-house and their home-made wines, particularly the rich elderberry wine which was like good port.

Brasenose Ale

2 PINTS ALE
2 CLOVES
PINCH OF GROUND NUTMEG
SUGAR
1 COOKING APPLE

Before preparing the drink, bake the apple in the oven or in an open fire. Heat the ale with spices and sugar to taste until hot but not boiling. Add the apple, and serve hot. This was a traditional Shrove Tuesday drink. Lamb's Wool was a similar drink served on November 1st, named after "La Masubal", the angel presiding over fruit and seeds. The drink is made from equal quantities of ale and white wine, heated with nutmeg, cinnamon and sugar, with roasted crab-apples floating on the surface.

Spiced Cider

4 PINTS SWEET CIDER
3 SLICES LEMON
¼ oz CLOVES
¼ oz CINNAMON STICK
½ oz ALLSPICE BERRIES
SUGAR
1 SLICE TOAST

1 · Heat the cider with lemon slices, spices and sugar to taste.

2 · Cut the toast into squares, add to the mixture and stir well. Serve very hot.